Drops of Ink

Trials of the Endurer

anthony briscoe

LIFE TO LEGACY

ISBN 978-1-947288-52-2

Printed in the United States
10 9 8 7 6 5 4 3 2 1

Published by Life To Legacy, LLC
P.O. 1239
Matteson, IL 60443
877-267-7477
www.Life2Legacy.com
Life2legacybooks@att.net

Cover & Interior Design:
Forerunners Ink Writing & Design
www.forerunnersink.com
jluvert@forerunnersink.com

Contents

66 RELATIONSHIPS

81 MY SISTERS

93 MAN DOWN

Foreword

An irreversible, monumental event we uniformly refer to as The Renaissance forever transformed not only the European continent but all of Western civilization. That event electrified science and philosophy, religion and spirituality, as well as the arts and literature. That historical lightning strike was spearheaded by courageously creative individuals whose prowess and insight had shattered the carefully crafted confines of a hopelessly oppressed world in the vice grip of the Dark Ages. The Renaissance was a sunrise never before seen by humankind.

Likewise, the dawn has broken the thick night once again, and this time upon a culture mired in mediocrity as well as a kind of collective multiple personality disorder from individuals trying too hard to emulate everyone else. Bravery in originality is sorely needed, and hearts of the hungry have long yearned for a new kind of artistic journey.

At last, the hour has arrived for the ones that have endured this hour of wasted jots and blots of ink, who have outlasted the assault of the average and mundane, who steadfastly waited for one whose poetic voice speaks to the soul, to any—but every—human being. Poetry is literature's music; poetry is the song of heart and mind, and Anthony Briscoe—The Endurer—is the esteemed conductor of his own unique concerto for the human spirit.

I have had the joy of knowing Anthony for about six or seven years, and I can definitely say that I have been the greater beneficiary of our friendship. He is an individual whose exuberant creativity is truly infectious; I regularly walk away from our time together with new ideas, new thoughts, accompanied by a desire to nurture and develop them. If I had to rely on just one description of Anthony, I would assign to him the same title Mel Gibson ascribed to the proud Scots that fought the English at the end of Braveheart: Warrior-Poet. Most assuredly, Anthony is a fierce warrior for Jesus Christ, his Lord and God, and for his family, whom he loves more than just to die for but to live for. (How a man treats his wife and children speaks far louder than what a man does at his job, in his church, or anywhere else.) Trust is fragile in this cold age, but Anthony is a man I trust with my own children. I thank our God for him, for his beautiful Proverbs 31 wife, and for his delightful daughter. They all have a special place in my heart.

I must say that **Drops of Ink** is a long time coming. This poetic opus has seen a considerable delay: not from procrastination or fear but from a sincere desire to see it done right and in excellence as all things a Christian man is to do. We learned that from a great man named Arthur M. Brazier.

So now my brother has distilled his joys and triumphs, love and affections into a masterpiece for the ages while having not withheld from us his sojourns in dark fjords filled with the icy waters of fear and disappointment; truly, what poet is worthy of the title if he fails to speak to the totality of the human condition through rhythmic verse? I'd like to think myself a poet having written pieces over the years, but nothing I have ever done compares to the prolific exercising of pure skill displayed by Anthony Briscoe. He respects and honors the traditions of the art but fearlessly forges forward to place his own indelible stamp on what will surely be a time capsule for future generations that sufficiently captures the cadence of this present time and the deeply rich colors and hues of his heart, mind, and spirit.

Gary Barnard Dotson
Author, Minister, Educator

Acknowledgments

This has been a life journey since my first book was destroyed by a source that will remain unnamed. In that destruction, the Lord rose up new creations—challenging, controversial, revealing, intimate but most of all hard truth.

- To my Father in Heaven who has granted me eternal life through the grace of His son, my Lord and Savior Jesus Christ. I can take no credit for this work, it is all your hand leading, guiding and crafting.
- To LaRita "Blessing" Briscoe, my wife and beloved. You are truly the enhancement of my life. Your strength, encouragement, prayers, love, and long-suffering have been the essence of godly peace and challenge in my life. To my Journey, you sacrifice so much of our time. Know that Daddy will do better in being there for you. I love you, love.
- To my brother Kenny B. Keep fighting. I've learned so much from your trials. Go with God always.
- To Arlene Jones, my cousin and first foster mom. I can't wait to see you in glory. You beat me there but I will meet you there. Thank you for giving me a chance to live.
- To Mother Wells. I don't think I'll ever meet a love stronger or more enduring than yours on this planet. It's because of the love you taught me that I am the man I am today. I pray you grow in His love that yours will become even greater.
- To Roscoe Jones, my brother from another mother. You know the rest, sir.
- To my mentors: Ronald Smith Sr., Leola Stuttley, the sainted Bishop Arthur M. Brazier, Tracey King, I love you dearly.
- To my spiritual mothers: Granada Cartwright, Tytrea Baker, and Carolyn Ferguson. Thanks for guidance, love, direction, correction, and possibili-

ties.

- To my P.O.E.T Family. Thank you for accepting me as I am and allowing me to flow as I am called to flow. Blaq Ice, ToyAnn, Double G, Tap, Jbutta, Imani, and the entire family that I can't possibly name, I love you all.
- To three ladies whose love and devotion to godly men burn deep in my heart.

  - Jennifer LuVert: She took on this project, came up with a plan, and deadlines. Thank you for your investment in me, I assure you it will not return void. Thank you for your creativity and for sacrificing your time and talent.
  - Jessica Lee-Cole: One of my oldest and dearest friends, the world's best kept secret. Thank you for a friendship that will never die. Thank you for keeping my works safe when tragedy struck. Thank you for your words of affirmation and resilience. You are loved. Deuces J-Cole.
  - Victoria Augustin: Well, what can I say? I wrote a personal piece for you that expresses how the Briscoes feel about you. You pray so hard, love so deep, share so real, and bless so abundantly. Thank you for cyphering through these works earnestly and adding valuable input.

- Intercessory Prayer Warriors Wilda and Stephanie, and the sainted Jackie Dixon, thanks for encouraging me. I know this is fifteen years late, but God's time is not ours.
- Dr. Byron T. Brazier, thank you for allowing God's gift to flourish to the masses. You are greatness in the making, sir. Be encouraged. Love you, First Lady Brazier!

Personal

41 years old, no degree, living check to check with a wife who stays home to homeschool our daughter, how did I get here?

Some say it was lack of preparation, I say truth
Some say maybe it was because Mom and father left me, I say no excuse
Some say, *Don't be so hard on yourself, maybe it was the abuse*
I say, *Don't get it confused, God has called me to be here*

See, I was told to act good, but since my ACT score was not that good
And one point growth from junior to senior year from a 10 to an 11
A teacher said, *You're not smart enough to be anything but hood*
But hood wasn't in me; I was destined for greatness

My path did not lead to basketball courts, football fields, or college dorms
It wasn't the community where gangs were formed and drugs were norm … No
God built me something special with will and wit to take on the devil
But with no guidance and no mentor and no direction
I became my own insurrection
Because without a vision the people perish
And unless you have something to respect, you'll never have anything to cherish
So while others committed themselves to guns and crooks
I picked up a pen in the mail room of my job in 1992
And I began to take notes from all the corporate hands that I shook

But it was strange looking up and seeing time fly by
Because it's so hard to see the truth when you choose to live a lie
Was life worth living or worth working
And with the core of a soul so damaged was my heart worth searching

What is your purpose, your dreams, your goals?
Keep them alive by living with hope,
Dreaming with vision, staying the course
Know that life, you were made for this and college, you were born for this, and
No man is your master; master all that you set out to accomplish
Don't wait until it's too late to believe you are worthy of your work
Never wake up with regret, but be grateful for each investment in your life
Or wake up at 41 with a mentor who is a 30-something-year-old Cornell Graduate
As your boss but at the core is a friend Helping me believe that
At 41 life still exists, and I can dream again

Learn to give and you will never have to borrow
Learn to love and you will never have to hate
Learn to live and you will never have to survive

Remember that being rich in spirit is better than being rich in money
But both should always be your goal
Live long, trust God, and enjoy the journey

ALL YOURS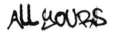

There's a distance growing between us, and I blame it on YOU
See how long do you think I can stay in this relationship and just conform to YOU
Everything I put forth seems like all give and no take
When I lay down to rest, YOU tell me it's no time for breaks

I wonder if ever getting involved with you has been one big mistake
Now I sit here alone and my soul contemplates
When I met you, it was fabulous—make that fantabulous
I mean people threw darts at our relationship, but there was no stabbing US

Now it seems like friction is all that's grabbing us
See, you remain the same while people take jabs and laugh at US
When you first called out my name, I smiled with a big blush
When you told me that you loved me first, I felt like it was my first crush

So soft your words when you whispered in my ear
Told me to have no fear and that you've driven away my tears
And all my past relationships, you told me they didn't matter
Then I heard through the grapevine about me YOU started to chatter

Writing letters to others that YOU put on public display
I mean I thought you were all mine then I find out you're giving other people play
See, do you think it's fair to give yourself to other people
And tell me that only to you I must stay

Yes, you're causing me distress; see, I believe that with you I am blessed
But to see others react to you in ways that I don't is causing me stress
It's like you're loving them better than you're loving me
So you've spread your love around town and you're telling me to stay be

There's a distance growing between us, and I blame it on YOU
See how long do you think I can stay in this relationship and just conform to YOU
Everything I put forth seems like all give and no take
When I lay down to rest you tell me there's no time for breaks

So, I decided to step out on my own and step out of your home
Met someone that lets me be who I desire and puts no pressure on my dome
She let me have my way with her, let me touch her how I feel
See, you said you were faithful, but this passion is the real deal

But for some reason I ate a bad meal
Felt like treason with a little false pretense that left me ill
See what I thought was a blessing was actually a world that has left me bitter
And I want to come back to you, but I don't know how you feel about quitters

I found out the grass was greener on the other side, but it was a lot more to mow
And the seeds were of a different breed and they were the wrong ones to sow
See, God, when you told me don't leave you, I thought you said it selfishly
But little did I know you were doing it all for me

Drops of Ink

Please don't interrupt my melodic flow as I dance to the beat of an embryo
With memories of how it used to be, you know,
"Back in the day when I was young"
As I watched my aunt get high, strung out on heroin
That sucked the life out of the child she was carrying
Embryo be no more and my beat stops
My eyes pace as my fingers trace the scars left on her once-caramel arms
Where the signature of a needle did her harm

Remembering when my tears were covered in the rain when my mother left
Me and my brother but never came back again, so now I'm scared to
"Go outside in the rain"
Because I'm still drenched in the pain of rejection
Wondering if I'll see my umbrella again; see, Moms was our protection

Please don't interrupt my poetic flow
As I climb the mountain of my father's afro
that was natural with the steel, black pick
That made you "Pump your fist like this"
Yeah, Pops sho' loved his afro but never gave his sons a kiss,
Never granted a birthday wish
That's when my hair ceased to grow; I don't need a pick any more
I climb my own mountains with the baldness of my scalp,
Able to maintain the fuzz that remains

Thinking, "Back in the day when I was young" watching my grandfather
Force himself into my grandmother, watching him blacken her eye
And tell her that he loved her
I still slide down the tear streaks in her cheeks
Remembering when she told me to count my blessings,
But all I could count were her bruises
Prayed to Jehovah to take her pain away,
Then my pain came when He took her away
Now all I count are the memories of her and me hearing the thumps,
Feeling the lumps and counting the bumps
With clumps of childhood memories
That remind me of how the good ole days used to be

Please don't criticize me until you realize me and my poetic-melodic flow
As I dance to the heart of an embryo I never gave a chance to grow
Well you know how it goes: "We must be babies having babies"
I scream when I dream of a child saying,
"Daddy, you never took the chance to raise me
Never took time to let my mother carry me, yet you had no problem burying me".

13

Thinking back in the day when my brother took 43 pills,
A bottle of Pepto, and NyQuil
Trying to tell his life to chill 'cause the good ole days were ill
My psychiatrist asking me, "Son, how do you feel?"
Man, if looks could kill, I would have turned that mother out
But that wouldn't bring my brother out of his suicidal mind-state
It wouldn't remove the childhood scars
Of big brother and me being baby-sat in bars
Sleeping in cars as dung clung to our skin, wondering if we'll ever be clean again

Pick up the phone with no dial tone
And hear the murderous tales of how darkness prevails
When kids who were shhhh'd and told to remain silent
Became violent just to be heard and express a few words

Remembering when the darkness of the times corrupted my already sinful mind
Trying to be like somebody else
'cause no one wanted to hear the silent screams in my ear
Nor see the darkness in my dreams, nor wipe the dryness of my tears
So I got drunk off the beer of fear of feeling unloved
When family members called me queer instead of dear

Please listen to my pen touch the paper and express itself
Maybe the skeletons in your closet will start revealing
The scars in your heart that need healing
Listen to my pen as it strokes and curves letters that tell of childhood pains
To make the healing much better—
Please don't silence my pen; she's my best friend
'Cause there were times when I could talk to no one else
So I grabbed my pen and wrote "Another Letter to Myself"

Please don't interject your opinion of my lyrical precision and incision
See, you weren't there when the spirit of molestation made its manifestation
When a "no-good scavenger, catfish vulture"
Introduced me to his perverted culture
Preying on little children's innocence; it's painful to reminiscence of a demon seed
That took my heart, broke my body apart,
Then left me ashamed and alone in the dark

Remembering when the name Mother was ministry, when parents had chemistry
That wasn't my reality but the realness of my make-belief making myself believe
That Daddy didn't leave and Moms was coming back for big brother and me
Got comfortable settling for pain as gain,
Allowing deception to become my cover and lover
Too used to situation as revelation
Because circumstance never meant a second chance in the good 'ole days

Please don't tell me not to write reality like this
I don't mind uncovering myself if it'll give another deliverance
Please don't tell me to stop writing like this
I don't mind telling my tales to pull a child from his living hell
Please don't shhhh me because dark silence can spark a life of violence

Listen to the silence, see the darkness and feel the numbness
Of a poetic pen that has allowed me to "Breathe again"

FLOW

I'm not trying to figure out what went wrong
See, when I started talking about Jesus
I expected to be stoned
Expected that the day I said I'd live for Him
I would die for Him too
See, I'm in this till the finish—what about you?

My life was a desert, but He's my water
Lost in this land until He crossed my borders
Stuck in a line of never ending fast food until He took my order
Delivered me from the hoarders like a mail sorter
For Jesus I'm relentless

I was stumbling in life until I fell down in repentance
He put my sins in remission,
Those of commission and omission
My stony heart he changed the condition
Put my mind in a new position
Then I became a Christian, and He put me on a mission
I'm brother spoken word

Taking the Gospel of Christ to lands and areas that most haven't heard
Spitting fires in circles that most would find absurd
I rip that Hip Hop / Hip Hope, pure Christ pure dope
Take no credit for the words I spit because they are Spirit wrote

Satan is cut throat
Coming after you like Seal Team 6 after Osama
Like The Republican Party going after Obama
Like Atlanta Housewives searching for drama
Like Fox News and O'Reilly going after Common

But I'm not a common man, don't serve a common God
I need no one's accolades as long as God applauds
He can stand on His own like an independent clause
If I'm moving too fast, He says Selah and I pause—
He's all over me

Like tattoos on Lil' Wayne
He writes His vision on my heart and makes it plain
Satan wanted to accuse me,
But when he looked, back God already removed the stain
Trying to tell my young daughters to abstain from sexual sin
He's only your friend while he's in,
And when he's done he won't be back again
Trying to tell my young men to abstain from sexual sin
'Cause once you go in, the pleasure will have you going back
Again and again . . . don't let sin win

Present your bodies a living sacrifice,
Our Messiah is not a fable; He's a living Christ
Getting into your My Space and your Facebook sites
just to see how you virtually live your life
A double-minded man is unstable in all his ways
That means even your Twitter
And status page should give God praise

I'm not trying to figure out what went wrong
See, when I started talking about Jesus
I expected to be stoned
Expected that the day I said I'd live for Him
I would die for Him too
See, I'm in this till the finish—what about you?

Flowin

Man, I am not jokin'. Can't you see I'm broken
Don't you see the rain over my heart and how it's soaken
My back's against the wall, and I have nothing to hope in
At least that is the lie I believe when it is spoken
Crying every day, strugglin' when I'm prayin'
Try to share my heart, but y'all not hearin' what I'm sayin'
Handsome on the outside, choken on the inside
Flawless on the outside, smokin' on the inside
Faithless and fearful, weary so I'm tearful
Wish I had someone that could lead me to a miracle
Not about the job man, it's about a vision
My people so damaged, we cling to the prisons
The locks on my membrane seem so much greater
When I make some progress, along come the haters
I'm weak and I'm fallin', depression is appaulin'
Wanna start college, but life is always stallin'
Why is it so hard here, why must we struggle
Every day I feel like my life is on the hustle
Even when I speak up, they say I'm causin' trouble
They beat me in the ground and just leave me in the rubble
Tired of being damaged, smashed like a sandwich
Wish I had a brother I could just take a hand with
Yo, can I walk with you, hey can you pray with me
Suicide is in my mind, brother can you stay with me
Never on the down low, spirits on the down low
Need someone to pick me up so I need a down bro
Iron sharpens Iron so make me a razor
Until I'm being led to Jesus, the Savior

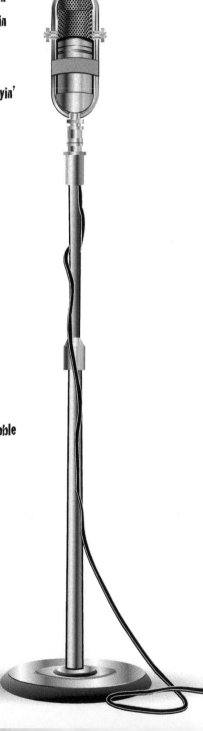

Glimpse

She was but a breeze in my life

A slight whisper

Leaving an echo

That would beckon recalls

Of a former existence

Not forgotten, not together

Needing shelter to adjust

to the weather

She's forever

A breeze gone bye ...

She was a mystery, one that captivated the infatuation that drew me to her. She was like math, something I enjoyed but couldn't and wouldn't ever understand. Her first impression left me hard, but mine left her wondering. She was private yet curious. Passionate yet refined. Attractive yet dangerous. How could she ever like me? I'm not her type, her brand, or her label. Not her words, mine, a wall built by rejection. But she had me internally. Why did we do lunch, and she kept me at bay. She was an enigma. Teasing and rejecting me all at once. Caring and nonchalant; vocal yet quiet. I couldn't stop thinking about her. Our attraction was before its time but a moment that would never happen again. The flowers I sent her were amazing: a tropical amazon that she would forever remember. Somehow she always knew how I was doing and where I was but she remained in the shadows. I have no regrets, my life is good now. The spirit of recall has a way of reaching out at just the right time to let you know that you were worthy of the past. Our farewell was enchanting. A bold move in to kiss her lips, a thrusting away to reject the love and ease the pain, a wave good-bye with her hand pressed on the train's window leaving fingerprints on my heart. The iron chariot signals departure. Farewell friend, the night's wind will guide my destiny forever. I stayed until her silhouette became a shadow, a vision and finally . . . *a glimpse*

I Miss You

Hey Dad, it's strange how God has brought you back into my life after all these years
Who would have thought that He'd answer my prayer and bring you back here
Into the life of one of your many sons that missed you for many moons
While standing outside of Mo's Pool Hall every day hoping you were coming soon
Held in Momma's arms from her womb, but I never felt you
So, I'm sharing with you a letter I wrote years ago.

I miss you

Hey Dad, you should see Mom: her arms are tattooed with needles
Her body shakes like earthquakes and she is always in positions that are fetal
Half the time she can't eat and looks real feeble
And she cries every time I beg to see you

I miss you

See, Mom buys powdered donuts, but she never shares those
I know she has them because there's always the residue left around her nose
But she needs to stop because after she eats them another man comes over
And her knees drop while me and big brother watch her mouth open to a man's crotch
Then we watch her pants drop, and she climbs on top saying, "Baby, don't stop."
But we have curious eyes, and we watch hoping that they would stop

I miss you

Hey Dad, you should see Mom's new boyfriend; he kisses me in the mouth
Smacks me on my azz when I take the garbage out
Tells me to be a man and makes me punch a two by four
But it's cool because he stops when he hears Mom's keys in the door
And he rushes to get one last touch on my thigh
It's good to feel the touch of a man since you're not here to be my number one g

I miss you

You should see Mom because she's passed out, and I can't wake her up
A syringe is tied to her arm, and I'm calling her name but can't shake her up
Maybe this syringe and needle I will try
So I can curl up next to Momma where she lies on the floor and watch
As drops of blood trickle down her veins
I opened her eyelids and her soul couldn't be found
Just a blank stare like I wasn't there, so I cried and put a blanket over her

I miss you

20

Dad, you should meet my neighbor's son
He's older and asked me to come over at night to have some fun
I said no, but my brother was gone and Mom said she had no place else for me to go
So I slept by him and he pulled my clothes off
Put Vaseline on my butt, held my mouth, told me to get in the shower and hose off
After months of this it became the norm, being left alone he kept me company
How do you feel knowing that while you were away another man was humping me
Since you weren't around to be my number one guy

I miss you

Mom's new boyfriend is a little scary
She's rich because he knocks out her teeth, and I know she'll get paid by the fairy
Strange, cause we all sleep in the same room
And when they are moaning and groaning
It reminds me of how my old neighbor's son sounded when he was with me
It must be good and meant to be; I wonder if he thinks of me like I think of him?

I miss you

Hey Dad, Mom's gone: she left us with friends and we haven't seen her in weeks
This guy is strange because he never yells or touches me or brother
His wife is nice too; I mean they've tried to find you
It's ok because we took them to where our grandpa stays
Since Grandma died, he needs company
They actually feed us, but they were weird: no needles, no syringes, and I think I heard them praying the other night
They reminded me of Grandma after Paw-Paw would beat her

Hey Dad, I'm not writing anymore. I figure after all this time you must be dead
I know my dad would respond to all my letters after reading what I said
I hope you are in heaven, I'll see you later
Take care . . . I'll miss you

Dad, it's strange how God has brought you back into my life after all these years
Who would have thought that He'd answer my prayer and bring you back here?
Into the life of one of your many sons that missed you for many moons
Held in Momma's arms from her womb, but I never felt you
While standing outside of Mo's Pool Hall every day hoping you were coming soon
So, I'm sharing with you a letter I wrote years ago . . . Welcome home!

Metaphor of Love

Close your eyes and see what I hear
Cover your ears and hear what I see
Leave my side and draw closer to me
Keep your hands to yourself and caress my body
Take a plane and sail with me to the land of passion
Take this pillow and rest your head on my chest
Go to sleep and speak to me all night
Talk to me, but don't open your mouth
Close your door and let me enter your love
Wipe me from your memory and forget me not

How lovely you are to me, my beloved!

Soothe my pain and let me suffer for you
Drive my emotions and swim in my affection
Clothe me with your desire and be naked
Show me no reaction and be shaken
Take my treasure for I am broke
Forgive my mistakes and trust me with your heart
Break me with your correction and mend me with your mercy

How lovely you are to me, my beloved!

Show me your strength and be weak
Show me your pride and be humble
Count my gifts to you and don't record them
Never defy your king and let me know when I am wrong
Disconnect your phone, but don't forget to call me
Reveal your love for me and keep it secret
For we are different yet the same
You are my metaphor of love

Moments with You

When the sun's rays blazed across your face,
I saw a subtle smile come across your face
'Cause you can sense my presence in this place
As the clouds moved past the moon, you found yourself consumed
With me caressing your stomach, trying to touch the child in your womb
As the stars moved over the sky, I saw the twinkle in your eye
When I lay by your side and whispered, "I will love you until I die"

As sounds muffled your ear, you felt me standing near
I turned you around, kissed your face, and drank your tears
When the rain danced against the windows,
I felt you shiver from my soft, gentle touch that made you quiver

As the planes hovered across the sky, I could feel you flying by
Standing by my side: my precious, my beloved, my bride
When the waves crashed against the shore, I knew you wanted more of me
More time, more love, more gifts from a man whom you adore

When the clock went tock, it was then I heard your heart tick
It was there I felt our child kick, wanting to meet us soon but not too quick
Wind chimes romanced the sacred night as I kissed you good night
Dreamed of a place where I could take you for the rest of our lives
I stood in still waters until you came with ripples
Your uncanny, undying, and faithful devotion to me is a riddle

My immortal beloved, my sunny valentine
Lover of my soul, body, and mind
For every day that passes in time
I'll enjoy moments with you
'Cause without you
My life doesn't move
My heart doesn't groove
My pain won't be soothed
'Cause I love loving you

How do I tame the **dark** within
I asked the Lord to give me this gift of the pen
So I can write and express what I feel therein
I can't live in the past, but memories surface again and again

How have I made it through all the hurt and all the pain
Even the sin through my life holding my head in shame
It's because Christ died for me, and now I'm changed
Took shackles off my mind so I wouldn't be deranged

Can you explain how others went through the same thang
But they became rapists and murderers and criminally insane
Not even my wife can dry the tears I cry
Only the Lord is safe for me to run and hide
Lord knows I've tried to write of His joy and all

But it's the truth that keeps me speakin' to y'all
It's His grace that lets me tell my life
It's His love that lets me share the Christ
It's His power that keeps me when I am weak
It's His mercy that covers me as I walk the street

Look deep in ya life while you're picking your brain
And you'll see how you overcame
Yeah, it's real nice to know that Jesus walks
But I find it better to know that Jesus talks

To me, through His Word,
That's where I find my peace for the dark within.
It's the Holy Spirit that tames the beast
My love for the Lord will never cease
Through tests and trials, I pray my hope never decrease
I hope to trust Him and that my faith increase
If my mind is stayed on Him, I'll be in perfect peace

I was dead without perfection while under the law
Now it's by God's grace and Christ's death, because I'm flawed
So it's only through Christ that I bring you my pain
'Cause He has taken all bad and made it my gain

my heart

I seem to have lost control of me
Letting any and everybody take a hold of me
Letting my emotions take control of me
Removing the Lord and letting things of the flesh console for me

See the Lord is telling me that He will be bold for me
That He laid down His life and put up His soul for me
But life has been harsh, and it's just too cold for me
So I dwell in the enemy's camp, where he just keeps scolding me

When I read God's Word, it runs out quick
'Cause there are too many holes in me
And when His angels try to minister to my issues
I resist cause there's too many foes in me
No one joins my pity parties, so I sit alone and just say, "Woe is me"
'Cause this warfare inside is like the folks and the mo's to me

I reach out for God, but then it seems like He's stalling me
Maybe that's because I didn't answer when He was calling me
Seems like the weight of depression just keeps befalling me
Satan is like a raging pit bull, and He just keeps mauling me
Could it be that I don't have the Lord's Spirit at all in me
I'm at church but not at church, and it feels like withdrawal to me
Some see my lack of spiritual growth, and they look appalled at me
My once spiritual highs have turned into spiritual cries,
Now there's a brick wall in me

My temperament is hot, and I wish I had some men
Who would just pause with me
Take me by the hand and patch these wounds
By putting some spiritual gauze on me
I can't trust my sisters
Because they just keep pointing out the flaws in me
But maybe that's my own delusion
Because I have oppressive claws in me
I'm wondering if I have the Lord's spiritual laws in me
In Romans One it must be art
Because on my heart He says He draws in me
Stuck in myself for so long, it's like a lock on my spiritual jaws to me
But I'm going to squeeze out a praise even if it's just "Help me, Lord!"

'Cause that's how it ought to be

I'm feeling a whole lot better because I found out I'm a King's kid
Found out that I didn't have to fight those battles in my own strength
because of what the King did
Told me that I must learn to have a heart of David
'Cause in His line is where the King hid
Told me to get back up after I fall
Because at times that's how Israel's God-chosen king slid

I serve a God who is faithful, so I never have to feel alone
If I'm quick to repent, He's quicker to forgive
So I will always have a home
And since Christ paved the way, I can go to His throne on my own
And with my problems that still remain
I can trust in Him even when they are not gone

Got power inside me now so I stand in the blood
Trusting in Jesus because He'll raise up a standard
When the enemy comes in like a flood
How could it be that He's there for one that lived life in the mud
How can it be that He keeps loving on me
Shen He knows my thoughts are crud

But I'm feeling a whole lot better, spending time daily in His Word
Laughing at the times I thought He left my side—
Man, I must have been absurd
I mean, I turned my back on Him, and He never kicked me to the curb
Waiting in faith, yet can you believe He never kicked me to curb

Yeah, this faith walk is something else,
Got saints walking with me so I don't have to do it by myself
Dusted off those old books on prayer from my shelf
Armored as a soldier of God, so satan ain't gotta go home
But he gotta go mess with someone else

Lord, I thank you for your patience and for loving a wretch like me
Never homeless because wherever I plant my feet you're always there with me

Yeah, I'm feeling a whole lot better 'cause the Lord has been good to me
Rockin' that ole' skool hymn—He's real 'cause He has given me the victory

Remarkable You

How can you love me?
Why do you love me?
My mood swings . . .
My attitude flings . . .
My anxiety that wrongs . . .
My worrying songs . . .
Why do you love me?
How can you love me?
My lazy ways . . .
My no assist you days . . .
My mental strain . . .
My words that cause pain . . .

Why do you love me?
How can you love me?
My rolling eyes . . .
My constant hanging with the guys . . .
My growing size . . .
Missing daddy-daughter time . . .
Why do you love me?
How can you love me?
How can you love me?
Why do you love me?

Maybe it's how I provide
Maybe it's my subtle stride
Maybe it's my goofy dance
Maybe it's my secret glance
Whatever the reason, keep hugging me

Not sure why you love me

Whatever the reason, keep loving me
But I'm surely glad you do
Not sure how you can love me
Whatever the reason I'm so grateful
But thanks for being you
Whatever the reason,
you're so faithful

Replaced

Time rustled by when the phone call came
Never realizing that forever our lives would be changed
In that moment, in the twinkling of an eye
An unwanted visitor named breast cancer stopped by
It was so hard to comprehend how this same breast
Whereby which my daughter was nourished, by which her health flourished
Could be infected by an unwanted visitor

How could this breast that I touched to please her
That I held as I squeezed her
Be now this symbol that has scarred the hearts
Hurt friends and brought pain and suffering still without end
How could this breast be now infected? Would I still love it or neglect it?
How could nature take what God perfected?

Keep it; take the pills, maybe it'll go away
Keep it; take the chemo, maybe it'll go away
Keep it; take the radiation, maybe it'll go away
Get rid of it and surely live another day

Time rustled by when she asked me if I was okay
I knew she really wanted to know if I would stay
Time rustled by when she asked me if I was okay
I knew she really wanted to know
If I would look at her the same way

Two things are gone: one I can't get back, one I don't want back
Her breast is gone, I can't get that back
Her cancer is gone, I don't want that back
But I am still here because my love is greater than her loss
And simply put, that can't be replaced

Unbirthed

To: My Unbirthed Child
From: Your Dad

Before you became physically formed
You were naturally torn
So my child, I await that day
When I see your spiritual form

Before I could hold you in my arms
You were subject to harm
When pain and cramping
Hit your mother without alarm

Before I could hear
The poetic rhythm of your heart
You were struck by death's dart
That also struck my heart
Tearing my world apart

I bought you clothes
When you were only three weeks old
I called you my child
Yet you, I'll never hold

I get tempted to ask God why
But I know Him and His sovereign will
So I pray, bow my head, and cry
And let His love dry my eyes

This is for you
My unborn child
Greet me at heaven's gate
When I walk my last mile

You should have seen me
Playing with the air
Tossing you around and around
Imagining you were really there

I had plans of taking you to the beach
one day
Kneeling down by your bed
And teaching you how to pray
Letting you go outside with your friends
to play
Following you in my car
As you went on your first date

Your mom misses you too
But she's stronger than me
She'll never question God
But thank Him in all things

So rest in God's hand
He'll surely keep you safe
I'll be home soon
Just meet me at the gate

Mi esposo amore

Dearest Love,

My sweet Aries, lover of my heart, mind, body, and soul: I bid you greetings. It was so good seeing you a few weeks ago. For that brief moment that we touched, my soul felt alive again. Being in your presence brought back memories of better times, of good times, of lovely times. You are my rock even from a distance. If not for your strength, I could not have raised the girls this long. My mother is well, love; she's getting better and finished her last round of chemo early in the year. Even in her broken body she helped me with the girls. She sends her love and her prayers to you. Somehow, I feel she knows more of what you deal with that you never share with me in your letters. If I have never said it before, you are an amazing man. When she suddenly took ill on our wedding day, you didn't hesitate to allow her to come and stay with us; and she's the reason I hold on to you. If not for her wisdom and guidance, I'm sure I would have succumbed to a nervous breakdown by now.

As I reflect on her temporary setback in health, I spent so long blaming God, but as I look at things the way they are now, it was preordained for her to turn ill and move in with us. I can only hold on to the fact that He who is Omniscient knew that we'd be in a place in our lives where I would need her with me. The Infinite One truly is Infinite. I am no longer angry with you my love; I realize that you going out that dreadful night could have happened to anyone at any time, this is just the cup we have to bear for the moment.

Our bedroom is not the same since you left. It feels like a cell, a place of solitude that I can only escape from when I am at work or out with the children. It is often hard to believe that this is the same bedroom where you made love to me, this same bedroom where many nights of intense passion produced the fruit of our womb. The same bedroom where we would kneel down and pray together. The same bedroom where we promised never to argue and kept that promise—most of the time.

The first year of your departure, I slept with the girls. Their floor seemed to be softer that a lonely bed. When I miss you the most, I immerse myself in their room, just to ease the thoughts of my heart that yearns for you. My heart doesn't beat the same, my poems don't rhyme, my songs have no rhythm. And if my soul didn't belong to the Lord, I would have no life.

The twins are still raving about their visit with their father. As I write this, they are with Mother making cards for you. It's amazing how much they remember about you. It is not me that keeps you in their memory. The way you loved them your first two years with them made you unforgettable. The many days you had to get up for work, yet would still get up in the middle of the night and tend to them and then check on my mother was beyond thoughtful. I do miss you here. They miss you here, but they remind me in my weakness and my tears, "Mommy, don't cry—Daddy will be home soon." The way they hold me so tight makes me cry because they have the same love, the same passion, and the same grip you held me with many months when I battled postpartum depression. You never wavered in your love, never pressured me for intimacy—you just loved on me. How could a man with that much care and concern be in a place with lesser men? How could a man with so much passion put himself and his family in this situation? I'm sorry, love. I guess my unforgiveness and bitterness still shows. Forgive me, darling. The longer I am away from you, the more my heart hardens. That was what made you special—you softened me. You were like my Downy that rinsed away my roughness. That is the downside of you not being here; a part of me is growing cold, and I hate myself for having such emotions. I am barren without you, a dry well in the desert of isolation. I just miss you so much. Archimedes could not write an equation long enough to measure my longing for you. No skyscraper could match the height of my love for you. My sweet, sweet Aries ...

Your scent is still in our home, and on some nights I feel as if you were crying out to me in pain—a pain that exists beyond our separation— like something is eating away at the very core of your soul, a diabolical plot to steal what is left of your family and friends but most of all your hope. What's wrong my love? What are you keeping from me? Surely you can tell your beloved all that you have had to deal with. Your letters are always so encouraging, but last night I woke up with an eerie feeling. I've never felt so enigmatic. It felt as if your life was drifting away from me.

I prayed and asked the Lord to cover you from the darkness that I felt; I know He answered my prayers because of the peace that came over me. Rest well, my love—it won't be long 'till we are reunited. I'll wait for you. I'll always wait for you . . .

A Force of One

Pastor Dr. Byron T. Brazier and First Lady Evang. Mary Brazier

There is the essence of a man
You look into his eyes and wonder
"If he were my dad, would I be in a better position in life?"
There is the essence of a woman
You look into her soul and imagine
"If I had her maternal love as a child, would I have hurt so many of God's daughters?"

There is the essence of a union
That breathes strength, courage, and some flirting on the side
When you catch them holding hands and feel their power
You witness *A Force of One*

There is the essence of a leader
Whose vision goes beyond future
Whose words uplift beyond recognition
Whose growth expands beyond measure
He is a man after God's own heart

There is the essence of a virtuous woman
Her support is second to none
Her intercession starts and ends with travail
Her love pierces the darkest of hearts
Her humility and boldness exist at the same time

There is the power of God
That places a mantle on a man
And prepares him for greatness to lead by example
And links him with a brave soul
They are anointed and gifted with purpose
Vessels to be used as the Master's tool

There is the thought of a clergymen
Where his ministers trust him
And he looks at them all and smiles
For they are the ones that stayed and stood by his side
When some left for personal pride
In the midst of transition and reposition
He knows they are soldiers, and they know he loves them
He calls us his ministers, and we call him our pastor

There is the blessing of an evangelist that is genuine
She shows no respect of persons, and that is why we embrace her
She holds no guile, and that is why we trust her

She harvests no contempt, and that is why we protect her
Her intercession is deep, and that is why we love her

There is the essence of a union
That only the Father Himself could design
Orchestrating the wisdom and craftsmanship
Of an articulate partnership that reiterates
The purpose of unity, faithfulness, commitment, and covenant
They are *A Force of One*

There is the challenge of a pastor
To reach beyond extension, to push beyond limit
To inspire beyond fear, to speak beyond thought
And to plant an inception into the hearts of mankind
That will raise a generation of lovers of God
To become the servants of humanity

There is the grace of a good thing
That breathes the favor of God
Her very presence is alluring and reassuring
She is First Lady, a visionary and heart for all
A warmth that supersedes her status
And she loves when we call her *sister*

There is the power of God
That intermingles two people
With two different callings
That don't overshadow the other
But complements their bond
And covers His servants for the work of the vineyard
And by His anointing, they will revolutionize ministry
Extending open arms to the damaged
And deliver a multitude of people
From spiritual depravation to spiritual prosperity

They have a connection in Him
Who has fearfully and wonderfully made them
To be covenant partners
Together, they will birth a nation by God's power
They will save a generation
For in Him and together, they are *A Force of One*

Awakening

In my own self-deprecation you have stilled my tongue
I take the focus off the impure me
So I can focus on the pure You
You are greatness beyond expanse
Elite in wisdom, holistic in thought
Glorious in wonder

Who can search your vastness?
Explain your wisdom?
Comprehend your ways?

In my self-loathing, You have stilled my tongue
And have called me Your own
To you I belong
The all-powerful searcher of my reigns
For in my unworthiness I see that You alone are worthy
How great You are
Hear my prayer bestowing glory to Your name
Make my heart Your home
Make my mind Your dwelling place
Make my body Your vessel
In Your bosom I nestle peaceful, resting, assuring
I find rest in You through Your Son
Breathe on me that I may see life according to Your design
That I may follow Your will and not mine own

DISCERNMENT

Who can discern what I feel inside
When so many thoughts rage through my mind
Indeed, I find no one who understands me
Only those, when I fall, who seek to reprimand me
Only those, when I am promoted, who seek to underhand me
Only those, when I break tradition, who seek to band me

Who can discern what I feel inside
When so many dark things cross my mind
Only the intercessors that encourage me to cast those thoughts down
But not those who wait for my soul to be capsized
Surely not those who pray and wait for my demise
Not those who say they are friends, but I know they wear a disguise

Who can discern the joy within my soul
Surely the Lord, which hath made me whole
Yet not those who poked holes in my heart by telling me
"YOU'RE NOT CALLED—YOU'RE NOT GIFTED;
YOU'RE NOT FAITHFUL TO THE CHURCH,
BECAUSE YOU DON'T DO AN ELDER'S WORK"
Can you feel the depth of my hurt
When I seek to serve God, not man, yet serving God by serving man
Still cursed by man, yet I am still called to intercede for them

Who can discern the guilt of my sin
The Lord, who forgives me again and again
But not those with whom I shared
Who didn't carry my burden but carried my trust
To their friends' ears just to bring me down again
Surely, those who took my pain and turned it for their gain
Just so they could say to me,
"TELL ME, YOU'RE CALLED BY WHOSE NAME?"
Leaving my face hanging in shame

Who can discern the Spirit that dwells within
Only the Lord, who freely gives
Only God's Son, who forever lives
But surely not those who don't believe
And not those who are spiritually depraved
Choosing to reside in a spiritual grave
Only those who are saved

Who can discern the things of God
Those who have the mind of Christ
Those who have the gift of eternal life
Those who suffer from stress, trials, and strife
And still have the energy to believe God
That everything will be all right
Surely, not those who have made God's house a den of thieves
Not those who use the gifts of God for personal use
Surely, not those who have treated the Gospel with eternal abuse
For them, there is no excuse and great rebuke

Who can discern the thoughts in my mind
Only those who fight to walk in the light
Despite their blight and whatever the plight
Those who sometimes do wrong but strive to do right
Those who trust in the Lord with all their might
Those who walk by faith and not by sight

Final Call

Apocalyptic rhythms pulsate through my mind
   While drum beats of cataclysmic vibes run through the streets
      Singing harmonious tunes of doom that will soon destroy the masses
      Bible classes teach of Daniel's vision of seventy weeks
        Mind too finite to grasp infinite wisdom,
          So I ask the Infinite One
           To show me visions
            After the coming of His Son

     Behold, I see a separation of the wheat from the chaff
       The suffering of non-believers who once doubted and laughed
       Oh, how the mighty will be brought low
         As the sound of the trumpet will decide God's final blow
         The world's final call, the start of Satan's final fall

As I pray, I feel the power of every demonic force trying to sway my course
    But I choose to fight, not to feed my flesh
       I ask God to take me to a place
           where I can feel the pain of spiritual death
             A place where darkness lies to the right
             and the left
              and hope is only in death

I sleep only to find myself dreaming in another dream
       Where I can't move but only see the suffering of the world to come
       After the return of the Son,
          Who was preached to the world more than once
    I see those who have been captured and taken
       To this home of the Dark Man
          I see the bodies of those who have been massacred
           in this place called The Dark Land

         All I can do is tell you what I feel inside
     Empty and alone, scared with no place to hide
Nowhere to run, no sun to shine, while I fight the war in my mind
    I feel like a man born out of time
       Will I succumb to this feeling of vacancy
And feel disgust from my own spiritual complacency
      As I speak to judge another man who just vanished before my face
        Never to be seen again on this earthly plain
          Leaving mind perplexed, leaving soul distressed,

leaving my thirst for truth unrest
All I can do is tell you what I see
In these walls that surround me and these forces that confound me
These powers that mystically recall prophetic warnings from biblical history
That none took heed, leaving me feeling eternally bereaved
Bars, chains, black suits and cloaks with steel yokes
Locking frames around my mind, striking everlasting terror

From my error to realize that this dark place may be my final resting place
This is the beginning of sorrows,
Regretting tomorrows that seem never ending
While the day of my final judgment is left pending
Is there not one who can intercede for me;
There was a time when salvation was free
But now I see the penalty
For us who didn't believe

All I can do is tell you what I hear thundering in my ear
The screams from this place called the Dark Land
Ruled by one who claims he's God's man
But who definitely has a plan
For those of us who now believe on the Son of Man
I hear screams that would make a dead man rise from his grave
I hear tears hit the ground like hail as my soul screeches like a whale
Being stabbed by poachers, like flesh ripped apart by vultures
No mountain to hide me, no Savior to guide me

All I can do is tell you what I smell: burning flesh that prays for Sheol
Brutalized flesh that prays for Hades
I smell death for those like me
Who passed up living water for a remedy
The scent of those who didn't repent
Becomes the terror of those who gave consent
To receive the mark of the Dark Land
Ran by a Dark Man who pretended to walk
With light in his hand
But carried peaceful deception as a weapon

All I can do is tell you what I fear
When my time comes close, I feel I'll be punished the most
Because I have refused to bow to the yoke of this wicked Dark Land
Refused to take the mark of the Dark Man
I fear the screams I hear will become my own
And death's scent will become my own stench

As I pray to be awakened from this dream by a pinch
All I can do is tell you what I read, of tribulations never known to this land
As the book of Revelation unfolds before the nation
Before the year of completion,
The earth will cry with blood and get no answer
It will cry out with pain and get no relief
It will cry out with great travail,
Feeling the wrath of the one who said,
"Be not deceived; God is not mocked"
Therefore, my soul shall reap for my sowing of unbelief

Visions of apocalyptic rhythms
Pulsate through my dreams
As I awake to the wrath that rested 69 weeks
And on the 70th pulled off
The sheets of grace that covered the earth's face,
Now I rest in a solitude place
This hurtful place called the Dark Land ran by a Dark Man
Exodus—exit us, with no fuss
I see the bodies of men and women
That have turned to dust
That have been crushed, left to erode like rust
Salvation for us is only in death; peace is only in the grave
But my eternity is in question: does Gahanna await me
Still, I refuse to take the mark of this Dark Land ran by a Dark Man
To the God I rejected, my fate is now in your hand

No bread of life to quench the hunger of my soul
As I reminiscence of my mother's prayers I wish I believed
Of my grandmother's songs I wish I could hear
Of my preacher's invitation I wish I could accept
My good deeds couldn't save me; my kind heart couldn't keep me

But I know that judgment will definitely seat me
In this place where darkness covers my soul
I look into the eyes of others just like me
Who now know that unbelief was our sin
And that unbelief has possibly become our end

Visions of apocalyptic rhythms pulsate through my dreams
As I awaken in screams of sweat with a bed soaked and wet
Realizing that I am not dead yet
But stuck in my mind are the images of a holding place
That keeps a grin on Satan's face

A place where those who were deceived
And waited too late to believe
Will find themselves nestled in pain
Take heed now and don't reject Christ again
For no man knows the hour (get ready), nor the day (get ready)
The Son of man will remove His Spirit from this land
No light leaves darkness as Revelation unfolds on all nations

Apocalyptic rhythms pulsate through my mind
While drum beats of cataclysmic vibes run through the streets
Singing harmonious tunes of doom that will soon consume the masses
As I pray, only allowed to see a portion
Of Daniel's vision of seventy weeks
For it's truth you need, then in Christ you seek

All I can do is tell you what I know
No Christ, no life; know Christ, know life
Born twice, die once; born once, die twice
Visions of apocalyptic rhythms pulsate
Through my mind only for a time
As I reveal to the nations the Apocalyptic Revelation
When the saving grace of God's hand is removed, leaving . . . the Dark Land

God Is the Author of Clarity

God is the author of clarity
But those living by His Scriptures is a rarity
So I go by the name of The Endurer
Chasing after God ... **The Pursuer**
Eternal Security locked ... **The Ensurer**
Protected by His blood ... **The Securer**

Take His words to heart like arteries
He's been watching over me since my days in the Ida B's
So I spit bars that speak life unto resurrection
Spit flows to lead others to Christ ... **Perfection**
Destined by His call ... **Election**
Covered in the face of my enemies ... **Protection**
Kicked my sinful ways and satan to the curb ... **Rejection**
Sold out like a stalker for Christ ... **Obsession**

Laying in His bosom of love ... **Resting**
Still enduring the trials of life ... **Testing**
Never been a sinless man ... **Confession**
But Jesus is my Lord and Savior ... **Profession**

I Am a Worshiper

I am a worshiper, even if I come in rocking my snapback
I am a worshiper, serving the almighty God
And not living a life like some that is broke back
Sin in my life, Jesus broke that,
So I cling to the God of ole like a throw back
And the blessings in my life, yeah, Jesus wrote that

And I am a worshiper

Pants sagging, but give me time I just got saved
Tattooed skeletons on my arms and my chest, but I'm no longer in the grave
Used to throw them thangs with the GDs and the BDs
So this attitude you see is just the God in me
Purging the sin urge in me so I can remain

A Worshiper

Sold out like the kings of Gospel concert, I'm a Jesus convert
Working to remain transformed from the society
That man formed Adam left us all scorned
But knowing that for me the Son was torn so I could be reborn
I am grateful to now be

A worshiper

Not in lip service, not in shaking my hip service
Dropped my flags and no longer have to walk through these streets nervous
Because I am a worshiper

Living a life of influence so my soul can move people like an instrumental
Using wisdom and not judgmental
So a regular life of prayer is always implemental
And no matter how far I'm gone, I'm never far from home
For my God signal is always on, and I have 24-hour access to His throne

Because I am a worshiper

Not because of what He's done but just because of His essence
Solely because of who He is, I live in the Master's presence
As I keep Him first
He continually opens up the windows of heaven and pours out blessings
Even though when I came into the house of God
And they treated me like a peasant

I remain a worshiper

Why? Because he died for me, bled for me, and did rise for me
Why? Because when I was dead in sin, He kept His eyes on me
And when others thinking themselves to be wise and secretly despised
He saw the prize in me
Now His Spirit resides in me and His Word hides in me

Because I am a worshiper

I am thirsty without Him, mourn when I doubt Him
Scream when I shout to Him, excited when I talk about Him
My life not perfect but Holy; judge me but He knows me
My heart is deceitfully wicked, so His graces He shows me
In Shekinah He glows me, in Knowledge grows me
And because of Him, now rivers of living water flow from me

Even with my past that is stained
My mind that is drained
I am forgiven and Jesus living
For He has created me to be

A Worshiper

The Journey into Transformation

I am broken by you
Crushed beyond recognition
Reduced to a shattered vessel
Smashed by the thunder of your voice
that small still voice
Drowning in the waters of your rebuke
Silenced by the chains of your chastisement
Wounded by the arrows of your Word
Plagued by this image in the mirror
That makes me face a reflection that is not there
I am not real, a phantom of projected imagery
Shaped and molded by those around me
But you have masticated my apparition
Bound my conformity to self
You are an intruder
Searching me without permission
Pressing me without remorse
Purging me without regard
Shattering the dark glass that I once viewed so clearly
I was once comfortable but now I am in shambles
I stand in a jar of water and mud,
A mixture of sin and holiness
Unable to remain settled I am blended in warfare
I am stuck, immobile, and desolate,
Face-to-face with an enemy
You have revealed it as me
Centered in this conversation a great evil and fear arises
You have brought me to a place to examine myself through
Your eyes
For mine are still closed
I am quiet, waiting, longing, hoping
Transformation awaits, but my white flag will not surrender
I have made a dark banner that shields who I am
Then you came
With Your light
Your truth
I am ...
Exposed

Our Koinonia

You are the beginner of my birth, the finisher of my life
The allower of my pain, the reason for my gain
The cause of my stress, the reliever of my affliction
The forgiver of my sins, the cause of my convictions
The cause of my sickness, the healer of my soul
The reason for my brokenness, the one that made me whole
Words can't really explain who thou art to me
How can I put in words one who lives for eternity

The bearer of my cross, the apple of my eye
The drier of my tears, the reason why I cry
The lifter of my head, the redeemer of my life
The deliverer of my troubles, the cause of my strife
The Savior of the world, yet You died just for me
The one I can't see, the one I long to be
Words can't really explain who thou art to me
How can I put in words one who lives for eternity

Judge, Master, Mr. Discipline
The one who doesn't spare the rod when I'm walking in sin
Friend, comforter, the one who never sleeps
Whose shoulder I can cry on when my soul starts to weep
Words can never express one whose depth is beyond measure
The creator of all that exists—my Jesus, my treasure

The Called

Many are called to be leaders without knowing their power
Many are called to be servants because they realize their power
And then there is the embodiment of both individuals
They have the heart of a shepherd, an example of leadership and tenacity
With a message and calling to share the Gospel of Jesus the Christ
And with that you are empowered to move by the Holy Spirit
To take on the mantle of service toward dedication, presentation, and revelation
To show forth the Father's divine manifestation of strength in the Army of the Lord
The call is to pastor, the walk life is holiness:
In season, out of season one must embrace the knowledge of the scripture
And reveal to the heart of men
Their purpose, their election, their destiny, and their future
They will be challenged, ostracized, forgotten, mocked
And yet, you shall remain focused, resilient, and bold
Because they only have one purpose
And that is to preach the Gospel of Jesus Christ
They shall be tried, tested; they will fall and be perfected
And from those that once called you brother or sister;
They shall be disrespected and rejected
But none of these things shall move them for they are after God's own heart
And God will bless and prosper their way
Their heart must be for His sheep that they have been given charge over
Their love must be solely driven by the Blood of Christ
For anything else is an attack of Satan to destroy the work of the children of God
Your ordination, though commenced by men,
Is orchestrated and sanctioned by the Living God
And it is He Himself that has made your Election and Calling sure
He is your all sufficient one, and you owe all to Him
And for that, He will give all to you:
Pressed down, shaken together and running over
Each man is given a measure of faith, yet for your journey
I will give you My measure of Faith
To go where men have not flocked, to preach where most have not shared
To pray where men will not stand, to fight where men will not rise
To bleed where men will not endure pain, to suffer where men will run from trials
You are my servant, and my pronouncement is only of excellence
Forget the past; praise Me in the present and worship Me for the future
I am your God and you are my chil—you are my Chosen one

The Depth of Forgiveness

If they wrong you, will you right them?
If they curse you, will you sing hymns
If they stress you, will you bless them?
If they cheat you, will you test them?

    If they stone you, will you build them up?
    If they starve you, will you fill them up?
    If they hate you, will you love them back?
    If they short you, will you pick up their slack?

If they blind you, will you help them see?
If they bind you, will you set them free?
If they scold you, will you give them praise?
If they steal from you, will you give them pay?

    If they hurt you, will you heal their pain?
    If they betray you, will you love them the same?
    If they make you cry, will you dry their tears?
    If they scare you, will you calm their fears?

If they break you, will you make them whole?
If they take you, will you let them go?
If they neglect you, will you give them attention?
If they control you, will you walk in submission?

    If they confuse you, will you give them clarity?
    If they make you sad, will you give them hilarity?
    If they wrong you, will you right them?
    If they stone you, WILL YOU FORGIVE?

The Harvest

The harvest is plenty, but the laborers are few
Twenty percent are doing all the work, and eighty percent are glued to the pew
So this year, God is asking *What are you willing to do?*
The streets are filled with violence
Yet you complain the church is filled with silence
So this year, God is asking, *What are you ready to do?*
He needs soldiers who are equipped and ready for battle
Who won't be moved by every rumor or murmuring rattle
Those who have gone through training and are prepared are who He seeks
For this assignment is for the meek but not for the weak
We've spent long enough on our knees praying
But when God said move, we never got on our feet
So He's asking, *Is your heart ready to be used?*
There are no accolades coming for your service
No public rewards for your diligence
And for those that hurt you on the battlefield
No room for your heart to have vengeance
For the call is for those who are ready to lay down their lives,
So Christ may be lifted up
Is that you?
Or are you like those when Jesus said "Eat of my flesh"
Shall you walk away too
For the harvest in plenty, but it's ripe for the plucking
We do a whole lot of finger pointing
But when God needs servants we start ducking
When it's time for an assigned task
We end our prayer in Amen, just before the Holy Spirit can ask
What are you willing to do?
But He sees you, those who are here for Sunday school at eight o'clock
He sees you, those who are here for Bible class at eight o'clock
He sees you, those who are in their communities holding down the block
He sees you, those who have a heart dedicated to the call without punching a clock
He sees you, what you've endured through life with a once battered soul
He sees you, what you're enduring now when hardship has taken its toll
The Enemy has hit sights set to destroy our mission
We've put our lips against the angels of God's house
And not once have we asked, "Lord how can we support the vision"
We've become so self-centered, you'd think we shed the crimson
While those who are feeding the homeless

Are the same ones in the nursing homes and prisons
So saints, are you ready to move?
As we are in a place of spiritual transition
Watchmen, arise to the wall and take your rightful positions
Cover those who may not see clearly
But are trusting God with hearts to serve and ears to hear
For those in this Christian number
It is time to awaken from our slumber
And let the world see that the God we serve is a wonder
Are you ready for the journey
Then give Him praise for what He's done
Are you ready for the battle
Fret not because it's already been won
Lift up your hands and plant your feet for this course
For the Kingdom suffereth violence
And the violent take it by force
But the meek in heart shall inherit the earth
So Father, we thank you for strength and courage

To move without fear
To love without condition
To stand without falling
To encourage without condemning
To exhort without envy
To serve without regret
To challenge without judging
To endure without remorse
To witness without shame
To help without reciprocation
To minister without titles
To fight without fist
To preach without reserve

All for Your glory!
Servants of the Most High!
It is time . . . to come forth!

The Journey into Transformation II:
The Wall

I sit and hold your light in my hand
When I try to cover it, I am burned
When I let it shine, it heals
When I let it saturate, it reveals
A thought, a time, a space to behold your wonder
I have been so far from you, and you continue to break me
Visions not written, dreams deferred, goals not pursued
Trusting you partially has left a scarred me
Procrastination has devoured that path I was to shape for others
Yet you have known this and ask me, "Why haven't I shown this?"
No answer for this wall of fear was easy to build
But takes years to tear down
Cemented with falsehood, sealed with confusion, coated with deception
And I am simply not worthy of this journey
You still call me by name, and I am shameful
How can you pour new wine into old wine skins
Renew me, I am old; refresh me, I am parched
Strengthen me, I am fragile; conform me, I am impressionable
Seated in fear, I desire to be released from myself
But we've been together for so long, marred by conjunction
Unable to function as spiritual darkness clings like suction
Your light is in my hand
When I try to conceal it, it burns
When I let it shine, it reveals
When I let it saturate, it heals
When I let it cover, it shields
Purge me, rebuild me . . . one brick at a time

I was told there was one who came to save my soul
> *So, I fall to my face and attempt to embrace something called grace*

I fall to my face and pray to the one whose name I do not know
> *Hoping, if he's there, his face he'll show*

How do I call on what I've never known or rely on what I've never tried
> *You that presence I feel beside me,*

That disturbs the darkness that rests inside me

> *I was told I was born into sin and that I must be born again*

When I'm born again, will this cancer called sin continue to dwell therein
> *Will this captive be set free from the chains that entangle me*

Are you the one who can wash my sins away,
> *Even after years of living my own way*

What power do you possess to suppress the other member in my will
> *Whose voice is not small and still*

But comes to rob and kill what's left of a soul
> *Who's trying to find the one who can make him whole*

Can your spirit dwell where darkness overwhelms the wretchedness inside me
> *Are you the one who won't allow me to sleep at night*

When I toss with fright
> *Not feeling I'm living wrong*

But knowing deep in my soul something isn't right

I was told of a man who died for me after he was unfairly tried
> *Whose own people denied they walked by his side*

Are you the one I do not know, who was nailed to a cross for me
> *If that be, why don't I feel thee when I'm on my knees*

If I try thee, will you make my faith strong enough
> *So I won't deny thee in the face of adversity*

I was told that you're the one who forever lives
> *If I only give you my heart and make a fresh start*

But how can I give my heart to the one
> *Whose name I do not know and whose face I cannot see*

For my faith only lies in the things I can physically perceive
> *Until I'm spiritually free*

It seems the harder I try to pull away, the more people you send my way
> *Telling me of the one who can save me today*

Are you the one who won't get out of my way
> *When I try to do things my way*

Are you the reason my family goes astray and my friends turn away
> *Just so you can be number one in my life*

Are you the reason for their treason and my dry season

I was told of a man who raised people from the dead
Who fed thousands with bread yet had no place to lay his head
I heard of a man whose name I do not know,
Who came to set free a captive like me
Though I don't know you, you still love me
But what manner of love is this that is sealed with blood and not a kiss

What kind of love is this that a man whose name I do not know
Calls me friend despite my sin
Are you the one who can make me born again
If so, will I have to leave all my friends
Who've been with me through thick and thin

I have nothing to offer thee, but what can you give me
To fight this member in my will
Who strives to serve self and whose only goal is to rob, kill and stop me
From reaching the one to whom I blindly pray,
Please show me your way, I pray
I was told you're the one who can make me whole,
Change my mind, could save my soul, purify my spirit
But I feel I have too much to let go

I truly want to believe, but my mind can't perceive
The manner of love you've shown me, I don't know thee but thank thee
There's something inside me that says you're the one
The only begotten Son,
But how can I forsake all I have and make you number one
In this world so full of religion, a part of me can't make the decision
So much to believe, but why do they only kill the ones that serve thee
To say yes to the one I do not know may bring me pain wherever I go
Does this mean they'll kill me? Lord, I don't have the faith to die for thee
Please help me with my unbelief,
I no longer want to be spiritually deceased
For you're the one whose name I do not know
But whose spirit I'm beginning to feel
That spirit that says you're real, that spirit that tells my flesh, "Peace be still"
I begin to feel a love that's real, that has raised a wall against my self-will
I feel your presence raise a wall against the enemy
That whispers sweet deceit in my ear
That for years has falsely dried my tears

Jesus, is that You—have you come to rescue me
For I'm dead and need you to raise me
  Dear God, can you save me
I no longer care what my eyes can't see
  And what my mind can't perceive—Lord, I believe
I come to thee on bent knees; please forgive me for my sins
  The darkness that dwells therein; I want to be born again

With my knees bowed and the confession of my tongue
  I know that Jesus is the Begotten Son, and He and His Father are one
And now I'm His son

I was told of a Savior whose name I now know
  So I fall to my face and embrace the arms of His saving grace

The Warrior's Cry

I cry tears that turn red; I let out a shout to shake the dead
I breathe the infirmities of the land in an intercessor stand
My eyes ache from the lakes of burdens, not enough time in the day to pray
Yet I stay consistent, repenting for a land that turns from God's unchanging hand
I can't see His face nor feel His glory; I wonder if He's pleased with me
I wonder how He carried the burden before He was nailed to the cross
The cross that now represents victory but before held a man
A man whose face was unrecognizable, not by Shekinah but by mutilation
A man who was beaten lame and despised not the shame
Oh, what a burden I carry

I cry a shout that shakes the waters, that turns the heads of deaf ears
That allows the blind to open their spiritual eyes, that shakes loose captive minds
I cry because of the nails He took, and I cry because of the thorns He accepted
I fall down in agony because of the spear that pierced His side
I cry out with a shout that shakes earthquakes, that drowns water, that burns fire
A cry that starves hunger, ends eternity, and strongholds captivity

I pray that the world not end; I pray that the Lord tarry so I can evangelize His church
So I can prepare the watchmen for the Lord's work, and I find none ready as He did
As He found His disciples asleep, I find the intercessors sleeping at the gate of passiveness
Embedded in the shackles of complacency, standing in the gap of emptiness
I weep with a cry of humility, for my boldness is in warfare, spiritual warfare
Looking to the hills wasn't enough, so my boldness went to the hills to get help
I cry because of the pain of the inner me warring against the enemy
An intercessor I stand; I won't take off my armor

He shed blood instead of tears; He claimed victory instead of fears
Still, I rise with tears; yet He rose with the keys to life and death
I prayed for an armor bearer, and He became His own banner
I prayed for peace in every home, and He became Jehovah-Shalom
I pray for a land that denies His call and prays for my downfall
Prostrating, I lay feeling beat, warring against a foe that walks in defeat
I cry with the voice of a battered soul, and He said not a murmuring word
Yet to Peter that was the loudest cry He'd ever heard, and I affirm not to deny Him

Then I recall those times I refused to try Him and realized I did deny Him
Those nights I was too tired to say, "Good night, Lord," I denied Him

Those times when I prayed my will instead of His Word, I denied Him
Then the times I prayed in anger, I defied Him
But I turned from my wicked ways, and I prayed and prayed and prayed
Until all rebellion went away and only the spirit of Christ remained
Bitterness became sweet and anger became meek
I fasted and felt my spirit get stronger and flesh become weak
I repented for all sins of commission and omission
Because the Lord shook up my spirit, to intercede was my mission
I humbled myself and sought His face, and He healed my land
For His time was at hand, and I glorified Him, an intercessor I stand

He assured me that my faith would not stand in the counsel of man but in the power of God
He showed me the power of His spirit by the many prayers He answered
Those He cured from disease by His spirit of healing
He granted himself through me for the need
Those who received instruction by His spirit of prophecy
He granted himself through me for the need
He whom the Son sets free is free indeed

So I don't need signs that read, "What would Jesus do?"
When He's shown me through prayer that worldwide Jesus delivers
He showed me it's not about how long we cry or travail
Not by power, not by might, but by the spirit of the Lord
We will prevail with the Warrior's Cry

Now I stand despite how I feel, because I know Jesus is real—the chief intercessor lives
He let me touch His spirit instead of His garment, and I felt a multitude of hands
That touched Him through me, and I saw the enemy flee and captives go free
Then I cried with a shout of reverence and godly fear, for King Jesus is here!
My tears flowed with mercy, my agony turned to grace, my spirit felt His glory
Deaf ears became perceptive and spiritual eyes were no longer blind

I heard and saw faithful intercessors in the spirit realm binding evil and loosing Jesus
Binding Satan in the name of Jesus, loosing Jesus, loosing Jesus, loosing Jesus
And we shouted, not of our own accord but on one accord
At the words we heard from our Lord Jesus and Father in heaven
"Well done, my good and faithful servants with whom I am well pleased"
As Christ in God and I in you and Him in us and all in one
I stand, we stand, with a triumphant Warrior's Cry as intercessors

The Warrior's Heart

His Blood flows through my veins
His Breath flows through my loins
He has made my heart His tabernacle
And has posed me with a question in my devotion
"My child, are you ready for battle?"

There is no armor for my back,
For He is the full-breasted one . . . My Covering
And this calling on my life was not my own will
It was set in motion before the foundation of the world
That I would become The Called Out, The Chosen.
I am the Ecclesia
Who shall answer the call of this mission
To spread the Gospel?
I have responded with a fire that He has put in me.
"Send me, I'll go!"

And this is not that which shall be easy
For the opposition against the Kingdom is great
But we do not walk in fear
For as our Lord has overcome this world
We shall also overcome
And prevail with The Warrior's Heart

This Heart that is called to be fit for duty
In season and out of season
This Heart that is called to be ready to stretch forth
Into the highways and the byways
To compel all men to be saved

The Heart of a Warrior may not understand the vision
But will support the call
Without wavering, without complaining, without malice
This is the Warrior's Heart
That shall endure hardness as a good soldier
Not being entangled with the cares
Solely of his own life
But being committed to the community of service
To which you have been called to serve

This Heart that will be hard pressed on every side
But not crushed
This Heart that shall surely be perplexed
but not left in despair
This Heart that will be persecuted but not forsaken
This Heart that will be cast down by the wickedness of man
But shall not and cannot be destroyed

For the treasure in this earthen vessel
That has revealed the calling of God on my life
Is able to keep me from falling
And present me before His throne
An open vessel ready to serve
With honor, commitment, and integrity
And because God is my strength, I will not be moved

This is The Warrior's Heart: the Heart of Jesus
He gave His life for me
Put His Spirit in me that I may have life
And now, this day, I give it back to Him
And answer the call to serve in the Army of the Lord
I stand with a Warrior's Heart
A Minister. A Soldier. A Servant.

Through the Fire

I feel the heat and the flames of the enemy trying to seal my doom
A fire that started burning when I was formed in my mother's womb
I can feel the depression and the oppression setting up my digression
A flame of generational curses
That has left our unsaved loved ones in spiritual hearses
While I walk through this desert place, the heat sings for my defeat
Flame of the flesh appearing stronger, fire of the Holy Ghost feeling weak
Though many times I can see no footprints in the sand
I feel the voice of the inner-man telling me
"Hold on; change is coming"

The Comforter abides forever, yet I feel Him never
Will there be no rain to quench the pain of this fiery weather
It's a mystery why these flames attempt to burn my land
For I've turned from my wicked ways
I seek my Master's face, not his hand
Though I know He's near, and I know He's real
I kneel, I pray, yet Him I can't feel

In the midst of the flames, I feel our mothers' pain
When heroin went through her vein
And flowed through to her embryo's brain
I take on the intensity of our father's betrayal
When he refused to be concerned with the seed of his sperm
I'm surrounded by friends that refuse to turn from their sins

Though he said, "Lo, I'll be with you always"
I can't feel Him in these trying days
I feel I fight this plight alone in this land
There again, I feel the voice of the inner man telling me
"After you've done all you can, just stand"

So pray is what I do, on my face is where I stay
In His Word is where I dwell, under His wings I will prevail
But it seems the harder I try, the more heat I feel
Flames so bright I can't see the Wheel in the middle of a wheel
Though I can't see my God, I see the face of men
Who'll burn for eternity, who won't repent for their sins
I cry out to my God to help and save me
Then I wonder why these flames are intense but can't overtake me
 In the midst of the flames, I feel the pain of my brothers

Cold because they had no mothers, torn between many lovers
Searching for peace in sin, blinded by the enemy over and over again
Even in the church, men won't take their rightful place
How can two put ten thousand to flight if only one will make the chase
Overwhelmed with the tears of young children's fears
When a man who claimed to be a brother forced them to become his lover

It's my charge to bear the infirmities of the weak
It must be the Holy Spirit that won't let these flames overtake me
When I feel I can't hold on, when I feel I can't stand,
I hear the voice of the inner man telling me
"I'll never put more on you than you can bear"

That's when I realized why there were no footprints in the sand
For Jesus was not walking beside me: He is my inner man
Now I know it was by His mercies I was not consumed in the flames
So I repent and be content in whatever state I remain

It's the inner man of men that keeps the sinner man from sin
Like Jeremiah, fire shut up in our bones keeps us from the enemy's clutches
I've hidden His Word in my heart
And since Jesus is The Word, He's hidden in my heart
Enemies and weapons may form, but seven different ways they will depart

It's the Christ in me that rises against the enemy
It's the prayers of righteous men that destroy the yoke of sin
Knowing we'll never again stand alone in the flames
Knowing we'll be saved by calling on Jesus' name
Just makes me realize that we are on the rise
Taking the charge to evangelize
Just when you think the flame of the enemy will take you down
Hear the inner man and His blessed sound . . .
"No weapon formed against thee shall prosper"

More Powerful Than You

I have caused havoc, wrecked lives, taking it all in stride
I had no home so in your body; I decided to hide
I've turned you from God and made you depend on man
Not realizing that all the cards were in my hand
Because I am more powerful than you

Your color means nothing, your religion may hold no qualms
I am a threat to your existence—see for me there is no balm
And I've seen you not be calm, giving the doctors all your alms
I still find it a mystery why you continue to sing the Psalms
But it doesn't matter because I am more powerful than you

I've snatched babies from your womb, sealed many with doom
Made the elderly beg for the mercy of an early tomb
I've made doctors cringe at the site of a syringe
I've sent the nameless to the famous on many a drug binge
Because I am more powerful than you

I've left children parentless and parents childless
Caused rebellion in the meek, made the strong week
I've nested myself around the cells in your body for a feast
Watched many tears at funerals from seats
Because I am more powerful than you

Or so I thought . . .

I couldn't believe how you fought
When you found out that early enough I wasn't caught
You prayed to the Father with faithfulness and care
Then kept living your life as if I wasn't there
Because you decided I'm not more powerful than you

When they shared the news your family gathered around
Even those far away decided to come to town
And when you struggled to get out of bed
You didn't make a sound
And that's when I realized I couldn't hold you down
Because I am not more powerful than you

I thought taking your hair would make you look sick
But you put on a wig and made it look slick

I thought taking your weight was a dear price to pay
But you looked in the mirror and said,
"Heck, I needed to lose a few pounds anyway"
Because I am not more powerful than you

You never complained even though many a night you strained
Had me thinking your pain would surely be my gain
But your demeanor stayed the same and your faith never changed
And even when you left this realm, your family stayed the same
How is it possible that I could not be more powerful than you

And though solution you've tried to find, and I've baffled many a mind
How could I be inside your body and you tell people you are fine
Maybe you're just one of those people who's way before their time
And today you've come here to see the end of mine
And what I thought was my work when I saw your body destroyed
Made me realize your joy and the spirit to live that you employed
I've come to understand that no matter what I do
You keep me even in death . . .
And that I will never be more powerful than you

Tribute to Bishop

I have loved the Father
I have served the Son
I have received the Comforter
I have run my race
I have finished my course
I have kept the Faith
I have closed my eyes
I am with the Son

I have loved my wife
I have anointed my son
I have cherished my daughters
I have run my race
I have finished my course
I have kept the faith
I have closed my eyes
I am with the Son

I have studied to show myself approved
I have kept the faith
I have run my race
I have closed my eyes
I am with the Son

I have shown His mercy
I have ministered His Grace
I have loved my enemies
I have fed His people
I have lived His words
I have covered by flock

I have preached the unadulterated Word of God
I have lived to fulfill the Great Commission
Baptizing in the name of Jesus Christ our Lord
I have fought for the weak
I have encouraged the strong
I have challenged oppressors
I have uplifted the downtrodden
I have prayed for those that despitefully used me

I have run my face
I have kept the faith
I have closed my eyes
And by His Grace I have gained a crown of righteousness
For I am with the Son

I have shown love for those that hated me
I have shown mercy to those that have stolen from me
I have shown peace to those that brought me war
I have given charity for those that gave me debt
I have keep the faith
I have run my race

Remember that which I have taught
By Grace are ye saved through faith and not that of yourselves
It is a gift from God
Remember that which I have taught you
In all of your preaching to get to the Cross quickly
Remember His words that were taught to you
To be steadfast in season and out of season
Always ready to give an account for the hope that is within you

I have run race
I have kept the faith
I have fought the good fight
I have closed my eyes
I am with the Son
I am with Him
Which holds the magnitude of the universe in His hands
And at the same time hold you dear to His heart
And still rocks me in His bosom

I am with Him
That knew you before you were formed in your mother's womb
And called you blessed
I am with Him
Whom time has not grasped, love has no limits
And truth has no opposite
I am with Him
Who is before creation was, who is beyond the present
And who is ahead of the future
I am with Him
Who is Alpha and Omega

Whose height is beyond measure
Whose worth is beyond treasure
Whose touch is beyond pleasure

I am with Him
Who kept me while on this Earth
That my faith would not stand in the counsel of men
But in the power of God

I am with Him
Who rode down in His sweet chariot to carry me home
So mourn not as they that have no hope
But rejoice and again I say rejoice
For to be absent in the body is to be present with the Lord

Rejoice, and again I say rejoice
For I am with He who was and is and is to come
Rejoice, and again I say rejoice
For I am with Him, the author and finisher of my faith
Rejoice, and again I say rejoice
For I am with Him who has said to me,
Well done, my good and faithful servant in whom I am well pleased
Come and find rest for your soul

I have run my race
I have finished my course
I have fought the fight
I have kept the faith
I have closed my eyes
I am with you, son

Relationships

beloved

So soon you are removed from my life
Like a thief in the night, you were stripped from my arms without notice
It was a memory, our romance
Enchanted with grace, surrounded with love
And sealed with a kiss of bliss that would marvel the heavens
Yes, our bond shook the foundation of the world.

Then suddenly, it vanished
As if a magician pulled you from the audience of my heart
And made you disappear never to return
And shattered the hope that I had to love you until the end of time
Your disappearance as silent as a mime
And I cry with the sounds of a chime
That rings aloud my mourning, your betrayal

You are more than a memory but a knife in my back
And a thorn in my side that I would gladly remove
If you would only come back and seal these wounds
That time will never suture and restore our future

Surely I have been deceived
But still believe that you will return to my arms
And whisper the three words that a husband
Loves to hear from his wife...
I love you.

And I will whisper the three words rhat would bless your soul
As if Jesus were speaking Himself,
I forgive you

And that would restore a covenant as Gomer to Hosea
And rebuild those foundational stones
That crumbled at the first sign of trouble,
Oh, how I miss you.

Because this house is not a home without you
The silence is eerie, no clicking of your heels
That grabbed my attention when you walked into the room
No softness in your voice when you said, "Hello, my love"

I am allergic to loneliness
  and I sneeze tears
    and cough agony
      and itch with pain without you here.

Sleeping in a bed that weeps
Because your absence has left our mattress unbalanced and my
cooking never reaches my pallet
Because your touch was my taste
And without you, my heart is bland as paste
If I could just see your face,
Maybe you would come see the breaking in my body
And come heal your man from these blues
That make the ancients tear their clothes and strip naked in remorse

I am bare without you
  a candle with no wax
    a match with no light
      a torch with no heat

Come home and heal your man from drowning in emotions of quicksand
But you are gone — invisible as air — and I can't breathe you
Could this love be dead because I grieve you
This desire unfulfilled because I need you
This wound unhealed because I bleed you
This sight unseen because I see you still
In my life: present, not absent . . . here, not gone

Return to me with the fragrance of your flowers
And the mercy of your patience
The calmness of your resolve let this love evolve

It was a memory, our love, enchanted with grace, surrounded with
love And sealed with a kiss of bliss that would marvel the heavens
And shake the foundation of the world
Then suddenly, it vanished as if a magician pulled you
From the audience of my heart and made you disappear, never to return

But my hope . . . still springs eternal
My beloved
Please
Come
Home

DEJA VU

I am here again, because this is familiar,

My desk, my chair, my work, my office have been refuge

The kids are there, and you are there, but it is no longer home

It is a strange place because we are no longer familiar

We are broken objects in the shadows of a forgotten relationship

A memory of a love that once flourished is now vanishing

With figments of an imaginative foreign substance called . . . regret

We don't exist in this realm of emotions; we only share a space that is dead

"Daddy, I miss you," I miss you too little princess

When are you coming home, I'm waiting for you

Tears stream from the loss of my seed;

It has been years since I have seen them

All they know is that Daddy takes care of them,

But I have abandoned their hearts with a checkbook

What happened to our love, how could it be so easily disturbed?

And shatter the dreams of those who said, "I want to be like them."

They are like us, following our example of divorce

Men have left their wives

And women have left their husbands for self-aggrandizement

And the seeds of the forgotten are forever with us

Shattered, screaming in agony as they now refuse to settle down

The sting of divorce has left them . . .

> unable to trust,
>> unable to dream,
>>> unable to hope

It has become, oh, too familiar.

discernment *for* her

If you could see into her heart,
You'd look beyond her reflection
You'd see the core of a damaged soul
Being broken by her husband's rejection
You wouldn't judge her; you would hug her
You wouldn't envy her; you would love her

If you could look into her eyes
And cry the tears she'll never shed
As she makes love to her husband while envisioning betrayal
And the other women with whom he's shared their bed
You wouldn't mock her; you would pray
You'd send daily blessings her way

If you could see past her bright smile
You'd see the sadness underneath
How she prayed for him to come home
After he'd been gone for weeks
You'd invite her over for dinner s a solid friend would do
Not pretend her pain is invisible
As if you don't know the truth

If you could see inside her passion
You'd feel the adeptness of her pain
Kissing the lips of her husband
Even though she doesn't feel the same

If you could see beyond her strength
You'd see how weak her heart
When others tell her to leave
But forgiveness is her part

If you could see her children
How they feel with Mom and Dad together
Then maybe you'd feel the spirit of her vows
Her fight to honor them, worse or better

And if you look deeper in the mirror
Could you see this person as you?
Could you endure the hurt and pain
The brokenness anger and shame
And trust God to see you through

Songs of Love

with Nicole Hill

I dreamed you last night
Standing under a crescent moon
As dense rays portrayed the attributes of your body
Sculpted only for me
You are my beloved

I dreamed you last night
Walking amongst a forest of trees
Observing your hair move about in the night's gentle breeze
I admired your beauty as you lay bare on colorful leaves

I dreamed you last night
Swimming in Saturn's rings
My oasis in the desert
Sprouting water from fruitless springs
You have made known the darkest things
You are my beloved

I dreamed you last night
Pressing your lips to mine
For with you I know all is fine
Your love is vintage like wine

In this state, I pray never to be awakened
So before this moment is taken
It was in the midst of our lovemaking, my beloved
I dreamed you last night

I dreamed you last night
Held you from behind
Caressing you
Inhaling your scent
Intoxicated by the smell
Undeniably you
Reaching me in ways I had not thought possible
Until now

Leaving me confused and breathless
Wanting you to touch me
Kiss me
Taste me
Be with me
Wanting to find comfort with you
If only for a little while

I dreamed you last night
The touch of your hair against my skin
Your breath against my cheek
The feel of your lips
Taking from me my very essence
Leaving me spent

I dreamed you last night
The warmth of your skin against mine
Our bodies intertwined
Dancing that slow sensual dance
Rhythms as old as time
Guided by instinct, feeling, emotion
Love

I dreamed you last night
Whispering in my ear
Private things meant only for us
Tracing the line on my collarbone with your tongue
Branding me yours
Muffling cries of passion, not sorrow
Joy, not pain
Floating, flying
Together

I dreamed you last night

My Immortal Beloved 11

I have yet to know your scent, but I know your love
It is wonderful in my sight
To love you is to love another side of God that I've never known
Your challenge for me to leave the past behind can only mean
That you genuinely care for my well-being
For that, you are my Immortal Beloved

Touch the hand of my heart and feel how it drums
To the rhythm of your soul
For the same Spirit of God that has consumed your life
Has also consumed me and truly
Jesus is our Eternal and Immortal Beloved

Behold our covenant and commitment to each other
May no flesh, even ours, separate what we have
Let love consume us and fate sow us in eternity with our Lord
When we leave this realm, you will belong only to Him
But for now, He has given you to me as ...
My gift
My blessing
My Immortal Beloved

Your husband,
The Endurer

My Love

When I first met you I could feel your resistance
See, I know you thought I was like one of those other guys
That came with one mission
To make an incision, leave a deposit, leave with the quickness
While you are in tears regretting your decision
To allow me to go swimming in your lake

To eat dinner off your plate
And leave your emotions shredded like wheat on your heart
Soaking like oversaturated Frosted Flakes
Yes, I could feel your resistance

And could I show you that I wasn't like those other guys
That wanted to bone you
See, from the moment I saw you I wanted you to know me
More than I wanted to hold you
And could I convince you that I wouldn't disown you
Wanted you to stand by my side so you could sit on the throne too, as my love

See your tears touched me and I started to write
They burned so deep inside my chest I couldn't sleep at night
From that day my pen started to take on a whole new life
Expressing myself in ways that I thought would amaze you
But I didn't realize the depth of your hurt
Was so bad that not even the truth could phase you
But still I tried

Not to tell you but show you I wouldn't abuse you
I wouldn't give you poetic words to confuse you
I hadn't earned your love and didn't want to already lose you
I'd never use you and if given the chance I would never refuse to
Take you as ... my love

But your heart needed moldin
Your hands needed holdin
Your arms needed unfoldin
Your psyche some consoling
And I was brazen enough to take the chance
Bold enough to make a stance
To get into your heart, your mind, and your soul
Baby, keep on your pants I just want you to be

My love...

Cause this thing I want built on a spiritual foundation
See you had kids and I can love another man's child
But what I can't be is a rebound to ease the pain
Of someone else's technical foul that made you bleed inside out
And make you put up resistance

So the days you didn't want to be bothered, alone I left you
Even with tears in my eyes because of your pain inside
It was my prayers that kept you
Even endured the stories of your mistreatment
With you crying on my shoulder
I wept too
All I wanted was the opportunity to bless you as my love

But you asked for space and I gave it
Told me your heart needed resurrecting
I told you I could save it, I would raise it
I could rekindle the fire and blaze it
So much so that by my love you'd be singing God's praises
For my love

But it wasn't enough
Feel like I'm stuck in part two of somewhere between hi and bye
And instead of singing "My My My" you're so fine
I sit alone and cry cry cry, wondering how could I be so blind
All I wanted was for you to be my love

But this man had a hold on your soul
And when you texted my phone thinking it was him
I began to understand that you had no control
Or better yet
I had to realize that I was trying to be your God
And a mortal man like myself had no chance of making you whole
Or for you to ever be ... my love

no keys

Do you love me, do you know how I feel about you
Not what everyone else thinks or what you desire
Do you know how I feel about you, do you even care
I know your mind and heart are elsewhere
But do you know I love you?

So strange our relationship, I know you have love for me
But when are you going to fall in love with me, I loved you first
All the things I've done for you, and I am doing for you
I can't even get a key to your house
When I want to get in, I have to wait until you unlock the door
But what about those times when I want to be wih you
When I want to clean your house and you keep me locked out
Do you know how much I love you; do you even care

Seems that everyone else has a key to your house
But I don't want a copy, I want the master key
I want to let you into my secret place
I want access to you whenever I want to come in
I shouldn't have to unlock your door; I shouldn't even need a key
But I'll take that key if you won't give it to me willingly

My Father said I should leave you alone
But I said, "No Daddy, she's got to get through this"
Do you know I pray for us daily that our relationship will grow
I feel the warfare you're in, flesh saying yes, spirit saying no
I can see the permanent streaks running down from your face
Those tears of pain and rejection have left a rumpled road over
And when I wanted to dry your tears, my daddy said no
Remember, she's got to get through this

So when can I come into your house
How long will you hold me out
Your love isn't ready to be given out
Only I can heal your love—don't you know I love you
Maybe you like the state of your house
Closet so full of junk and excess baggage, fridge full of hot water
Containers molded with old cabbage all milk and no meat
But baby, I don't want to redecorate your house, I want to tear it down

I want to break up and destroy every piece of that house you're holding on to
Cause in my Father's house there are many mansions
No squeaks when you open the doors,
No streaks when you walk on the floors
Just a house full of love, a room full of healing
A kitchen full of living bread to eat
A glass full of living water to drink
An empty closet to meditate and think

Do you know how much I love you, cause I know you really care
Just give me the key, and I'll throw it away, I know it hurts
But trust me new creature, old things will pass away
And behold, I'll make everything new
Because my Fath'ers house doesn't need a key if you have me

I'll take those tears of pain and turn them into champagne
I'll take that heart of stone and put one of flesh in your chest
I'll take that spirit of rejection and replace it with my affection
I'll take that spirit of resentment and turn it into repentance

Because if you don't know, I'll tell you I love you
If you don't know, I'll tell you I care
I'm your eternal love, your maternal love your paternal love
So I don't need a key to unlock what's already mine
Just trust in me, and I'll give you rest

What Happened to Us?

What happened to us?
I mean we used to be so good together
Storms would come, and we could withstand any weather
But now it seems like bad attitudes and screams
Finding more sexual satisfaction in my dreams
Because you won't come next to me
What happened to us?
I mean, we were the envy of other couples
You sang at our wedding and I spit the illest flow for our nuptials
And if you were in pain I felt it
Even when my mind was tweaking with a half deck you dealt it
Baby, what happened to us?
I mean, you would cry, but the tears came from me
If I was cut, you were the one that would bleed
You would say "Bless you" right before I sneezed
You were like asthma and I was the inhaler to help you breathe
And my guys would call you the number one dime piece
The beauty of my life with no drama, we were blessings karma
The Bonnie to my Clyde, the pupil in my eyes
The Michelle to my Obama
Then drama came and we feasted at his table
All the years of church
And we let Satan come right in and make us unstable
Instead of spending nights together, we just settled for cable
How could we go from being a fairytale to becoming a fable?
What happened to us?
I look into your eyes and see a stranger
You tell me that the tone of my voice makes you feel danger
Our smiles have turned to anger
As for our lovemaking, let's just say I'm not shaking
And I heard you tell ya girl on the phone
That for the last few months you'd been faking
So much pain between us I can feel us breaking
What happened to us?
I mean we would preach to other couples
Telling them to stand strong
And when they found out that we were separated
they questioned if even their marriage could last long
I mean, we said nothing could tear us apart
But that was the pride in our hearts
And maybe—just maybe—our light was actually dark

I'm trying to figure out what happened to us
Long kisses became a short peck
Long conversations became a short text
Mutual compromise became mutual disrespect
Our son is asking, "Dad, when are you coming back?"
And our daughter is asking,
"Mom, why to you talk to Daddy like that?"
What happened to us?
We went from staying at church to playing church
We would tell other couples we were going through
To give them hope
But then we were playing hurt
See we started our relationship in Christ
but didn't keep Him in our life
Now this separation is cutting deep like a knife
You call, I sigh; I call, you cry
Is there any way to get back to fifteen years ago
When you were just my girl?
And I was just your guy
Do you think we could wonder in
And find once again that ribbon in the sky?
Because I still remember the mental love
When I first looked into your eyes
When I put 12k on your finger cause you are worth every dime
Even when I was unemployed you stood by my side
I'll do whatever necessary to make it right
Can we ever start over
And build this relationship on truth and not a lie
Because no matter what happened with us,
I believe we can make it if we try, just the two of us—you and I
Can we start over and be friends
Can we get God back in this relationship
Cause I want to see you smile again
What happened to us?

E-LOVE TO THE BLACKFULS

There is a world that exists that is growing popular by the day
A way to decipher if someone is real or just ok
So to get our life on line we venture online
To see who's on line with hopes that our thoughts
Our emotions, our desires, our passions, and our dreams are in line
Looking for that E-love

And electronic it may seem at its inception they look for something electric
And if it's the right mix of Christ and Salvation, trust with no prevarication
The Gospel with no mixture of reincarnation
If she's willing, and he's able then God can perfect it
Looking for that E-Harmony

So when things get tough, we'll walk in the peace of God together
With no thoughts of harming her and no thoughts of harming me
That gentle caress that turns off the alarm in me
That smooth stroke of the keys that types letters on my heart
With alms to keep me calm
Baby, we are the perfect Match.com

And most would say that we found each other too soon
Not realizing the individual preparation that took place so God could make room
No jingles, there's no shame in Christian mingle as Blackpeoplemeet
From that first date, then second, then third, you made my heart twinkle
You put creases where I had wrinkles
Now our hearts are no longer clothed, you are my Pandora and baby I SEE You

Breathe you, need you, take your pain and grieve for you
Take your wounds and bleed for you
Consume me, Lawrence, until I am no longer hungry and I am Black Ful
Until I know all of your needs are met
To a point I fulfill your dreams without having to ask you
Spin me in your Charlette's web so we can stay caught together
By my side in trials so we can say we fought together
Merge our finances as one so we can say we bought together
Intercede in prayer for God's will, so we can say to Him we sought together

Father, we thank you for surfacing what no one can keep under
Thank you for merging what no man can put asunder
This is unity, this is marriage, this is bonding, this is solidarity, this is fate
Because the Lord has brought to life what started out as an online date

This is no mistake; this is just how it goes
When you seek to get your life inline, don't rule out what God can show
Don't stunt what God can grow
And as long as we walk in the Holy Spirit, we're simply walking in the flow
Now that's E-ternal LOVE

My Sisters

A Mother's Heart

So soon you are removed from my life
In pain I birthed you, in love I raised you
Waiting with anticipation for the day that Jesus would save you
I fed you from my breast and put you to sleep on my chest
Those early days when you were tired and needed rest
You are my princess, the fruit of my womb, who consumed all my mind
All my love and all my time

I thank God that you are . . . *my beautiful daughter*

I didn't know what being a woman was until you came
I was so proud to think of your name, my angel
I didn't know all a mother had to do until I had you
So I had to reshape myself so I could properly mold you
'Cause you are my baby girl, my world
So I never wore a skirt too short or a blouse too loud
A walk that was full of diligence but not too proud
Speak like a woman of elegance and make sure all you say is relevant
There are none like you, my child
For your smile radiates as bright as heaven's gates

I am proud to call you . . . *my beautiful daughter*

Look at you, my firstborn adorned in your wedding gown
I still can't believe that you're all grown up now
I cry tears of joy for I have watched you grow
I hold you close for I have seen you glow
Love as I have shown you, honor as I have told you
When he wants to console you, embrace it
When challenges come
Don't run my child, face it
Endure hardness like a good soldier
So you can pass it down to your daughter when you are older

God blessed me with you . . . *my beautiful daughter*
So many times we've laughed and cried
Stuck together even if we weren't on the same side
Shared words that built up and tore down
But I still love you, my daughter, smile or frown

We've fought like enemies and have shared like friends
'Cause you're my beloved daughter through thick and thin
I didn't always see things the way you did
But you'll understand my choices when you have your own kids
Never doubt my love for you that runs deep through my veins
I will always cherish my child, even when there's pain

For you are and forever will be . . . *my beautiful daughter*

In pain I birthed you, in love I raised you
Giving praise to my Lord for He so wonderfully made you

My beautiful daughter

FEANWOMA (FE-ANN-WOO-MA)
FEARFULLY AND WONDERFULLY MADE

Since the day God crafted man from the dust of the ground, I have been fearfully and wonderfully made. Since the day God breathed His spirit into man and made him a living soul, I have been fearfully and wonderfully made. I am fearfully and wonderfully made, even if the darkness of my skin blends in with the shade. I am fearfully and wonderfully made, created after God's image, descended from His spirit and NOT the seed of an ape. I am fearfully and wonderfully made, even if the whiteness of my skin blends in with the snow. I am fearfully and wonderfully made, designed by and after the image of the Creator to show forth His glow. I am fearfully and wonderfully made, no matter my shape or size. I am fearfully and wonderfully made, whether I have slim hips or thunder thighs. I am fearfully and wonderfully made, a blessing in Solomon's rose of Sharon. I am fearfully and wonderfully made, whether I can conceive or am left barren. Some say I'm cryptic and mystic; I say I'm gifted and different. Some perceive me as hard to understand—that may be so; can you still love me as I am? This is how God made me, intricate but not crazy. This is how God made me, relaxing but not lazy. This is me: a daughter, a sister, a mother. This is me: a comfort, a friend, a lover. Once you understand God, you can understand me. I am what I am, for this is how God made me. Since the day God crafted man from the dust of the ground, I have been fearfully and wonderfully made. Since the day God breathed His spirit into man and made him a living soul...I AM fearfully and wonderfully made.

Lingering

If he looked into your soul
He would see a secret that only you knew
You'll gauge his eyes and realize
This is love, this is meant to be

In you lies a mystery of intrigue
A question with no answer
A foundation with no source
A road with no course

The journey calls for you
It echoes off the corners of your heart
Purpose wrestles with fear
Destiny wars with doubt

Trying to entertain your worth
You shudder to think of three years from now
At this time, you grab the moment
Seize the day, appreciate the current

You respond to the image of night suns
That paint silhouettes across northern skies
You count the stars and envision a gift
A seed that has been implanted into your psyche
You awake and find serenity in the stillness of time
Yawning with arms stretched out you hug yourself
Smiling, you move closer to the inner you and whisper
"I love you, girl"

If he looked into your soul
He would see a secret that only you know
You'll gauge his eyes and realize
This is love, this is meant to be

Lydia

The essence of my beauty is not defined by man
It is not defined by people or things or groups or cliques
I am who I am because this is who God has designed me to be
Full of His glory, full of His substance, full of His grace

I am the called according to His purpose
I can fit into a box for my God is in no box
He cannot be measured, therefore I cannot be measured
No one defines my depth
No one controls my thoughts
I am fearfully and wonderfully made

Constructed, transformed the renewed
For this purpose I am come forth
To this generation, to this world, to this nation
To be an example of holiness, to show forth the glory of Creator
I am destined and gifted with a purpose
Undefinable undeniable and I am covered by Him

My destiny is to save man, to be in place daily
Ready when I am called, prepared when I am chosen
The mind of a servant is my focus and I shall arise victorious
For God is my refuge and my attributes will reflect it
My knowledge will display it
My humility will portray it
My life will show it
I am called out and engrafted in
And when He opens the door to greatness
I will live in it and the generations under me shall bask in it

For I am called for this moment to save the masses
And I shall be found prepared for the work
Fit for duty, prepared for service
And fine as can be for He hides me that He may be seen
He guides me so He may be shown
He speaks through me that He may be known

In essence my life is no longer a luxury
My worship in not perfunctory; my calling is concrete
This is purpose and I am bowing before His will
I will not be found an outcast, discarded for rejecting Him
I will be found in His service
Not perfect but undefiled, not flawless but holy. At times lonely but in His will
Full of His substance, full of His spirit, full of His grace

mother•daughter

Mother, have you seen our daughters?
They have been with strange men and drink from thirsty waters
Allowing any Tom, Dick, or Tyrone to cross their borders
They have sacrificed sacred treasure for worldly pleasure
And now measure their worth
On how many stripping poles they can grab hold

Mother, have you seen our daughters?
They run around looking for love, but it can't be found
They look for religion where the doctrine is not sound
See, they desire an upward movement but seem to be heading down

Bothered by absentee fathers
They have daughters by absentees fathers
Turning their love now for other women
'Cause with men they don't want to be bothered

Mother, have you seen our daughters?
Or better yet, Mother have they seen you?
Despising them for their youth
And because you grew up living a lie
You refuse to lead them to the truth

Mother, have our daughters seen you?
See you judge them for not giving respect?
But it's hard for them to grow in grace
If you raise them on invisible fruit

Daughters, have you seen our mothers?
See you judge them for staying with a deadbeat husband?
But she endured the hardness
So you could have shelter
And you didn't know, but while you slept at night
She laid hands on your head and said ...

"Jesus, please help my baby do better."

Mother, have you seen our daughters?
She had so many men running in and out
You couldn't hear the silent scream
When he covered her mouth to silence her shouts
See, you call her a slut
But it was your fifth boyfriend in a month that turned her out

Mothers, have you seen our daughters?
They are shouting to be heard
Daughters, have you seen our mothers?
They are shouting for you to listen

Women, do you know your worth?
You are the bearer of kings
Mary carried the Word for nine months
Women, you are queens
It's time to put aside petty things
Time to let go of the past or another generation will not last

Eve, come home and save or daughters.

My Sisters

Sisters, know that I love you
Break off any cat that attempts to backhand you
Back you up against anyone that tries to underhand you.
See, I know they call you Angry Black Woman
But most are not man enough to understand you
Or not black enough to comprehend you
So they portray you as this Amos and Andi Sapphire
But the last time I checked the history books,
You were Thomas Jefferson's only true desire

And to my sisters, I love you

And if we took time to explore
How you were forced to become master's whore
Then I would say yes
You have a right to be angry

As you were forced to let white babies
Suck the milk from your breasts
While your child cried all night
Because you came home
And could not feed him on an empty chest
Then I would say yes
You have a right to be angry

And the pain you felt when
They sold your husband
To a plantation in Virginia
And secretly sold your son
To a plantation in Missouri
Then I would say yes,
You have a right to be angry.

But **Black Woman**
Know you are the one who sustains me
And the way these young bucks, lil' waynes, and wacka flakas
portray you
It pains me every time I hear them ⸲call you a female dog

89

It pours blood over my emotions and stains me
And when hip hop births another lil' kim or nicki minaj, it drains me
But even to those sisters, I say I love you

'Cause I hear Sis Soulja saying, *Pump the black fist in the air*
And for every Angie Stone that called me "Black Brother, Strong Brother"
Surely you will birth my Heir
To every Jill Scott that sings to her Black King "He Heals Me"
I will lift up my Black women till the world either feels me or kills me

To my sisters, I love you

Forgive me for the times I treated you like a peasant and not a queen
Forgive me for the times I snapped for showing concern and treated you
mean
For every Queen Latifah that said U.N.I.T.Y
I stand and applaud
For every Esther Rolle that refused to become a coon for television fraud
For every India Arie that said, "I am the Truth"
I stand and salute you
For the love and sweet nectars of your juice
That dig deeper in my soul than a tree's root
I say to you that I love you

I take command of my emotions before I raise my hand to strike you
I take command of my anger before I open my mouth to spite you
And I cry with infinite tears for all the years
I caused you to shed tears by failed promises that I whispered in your ear

From this day forward I will cherish and hold you dear
So I can feel you by my side even when you are not near
Thank you for your forgiveness when I gave in to the lust in me
Thank you for the opportunity and chance for you to once again trust in me
You are the king maker and for my family you hold it down
So I stand because of your commitment and put on my rightful crown

Mother of my children, builder of my nation
I will shake the world's foundation until I feel the vibrations
Of your heart beating for me 10,000 miles away
And with every letter I stroke with a pen to show my love
I make this covenant with you and I sign it with my blood

You are my sisters and I love you

YOU ARE

... MY BIRTH

Woman, are thou the one who travailed in birth
To bring me on this earth
Are you the one who shielded me in your womb
Before I was born into a world you didn't want me to know
In the darkness of your womb, I saw a light like no other
For I knew you not as Mother but as protector
I didn't know where my bed was, but I always slept in peace
I didn't know where my food was, but I never hungered
Though my mind was just forming
I thought of a friend I'd already known
Though my heart was small in size
I knew you were true love
The cord that connects us spiritually
Is stronger than the cord that connected us physically
I knew when I saw your face
it would still be beautiful
For the love we share naturally
We've walked before the foundation of the world spiritually

... MY GROWTH

When the enemy would come and try to creep in me
Woman, art thou the one who prayed in the spirit
and stood between me
As I grew a little older, my pride grew a little bolder
You chastised me with your hand but loved me with your shoulders
When daddy wasn't able to be around, your love was always found
I felt the pain of your loneliness;
I carried your burden so you could smile
If just for a while, I prayed the Lord would relieve your torment
Again I looked into your eyes
and saw a reflection of a growing part of me

That would hold us in covenant for eternity
When my heart was breaking, you saw right through the faking
You placed my head in your bosom and told me
There's plenty of fish in the sea
But no one is good enough for my baby
Then I remember the love we share naturally
We've already lived before spiritually

... MY LIFE

Now I am your child, full grown standing on my own
But never far from you because your heart is my home
I look at pictures when you held me as a child
It's the same when you hold me now; you haven't changed your smile
Though many years have passed, we've shared joy and pain
Endured sunshine and rain, lived loss and gain
But the grace and love of the Lord has never changed
Like His love, we remain the same
As you get older, I pray the Lord will allow you to stay
But I know if you leave naturally, I'll see you again spiritually in eternity
If there were no you, there would be no me
You are my birth, my growth, my life
You are ... MY MOTHER

IN *Loving Memory* OF *Demario Bailey*

"You must get an education
You must go to school
And you must learn to protect yourself
And you must learn to protect yourself with the pen, and not the gun."
~Josephine Baker

Yesterday, while I was at church with my family
Celebrating the birth of Christ
I received a message from my school saying another student lost his life
And this time, as most in the inner city, it was Black on Black
Which doubly makes it wack on wack
How do four black men look at someone's 15-year-old son
And decide to rob him and end his life with a gun
And while some were down blocking off the Mag Mile showing unity
Satan came in again and cut down a 15-year-old in our community
No doubt these men where bastard child
No dad, no brains, no sense, no hope, they grew up as a hazard child
And how can I tell a mother that God blesses the child that has their own
When she questions is she still blessed now that her child is gone
What can I say to his mother, or what can I saw to his twin brother
What can I say to his teammates, whom he was on his way to see
What can I say to his teachers who encouraged him to be all he can be
What can I say to his classmates who no longer feel safe on these streets
What can I say to 20-year politicians that have brought no change we see
Hold fast, trust God, it's life, and it's hard
Hold fast, trust God, it's life, and it's hard
Be hurt but don't let it break you / Be angry but don't let it make you

Be confused but don't let it blind you / Be depressed but don't let it bind you
Be scared but don't let it hold you / Be furious but don't let it mold you
Be heated but don't let it control you / Open your heart
And let God console you
I can sing God Bless the child that's got his own
But what can I say to a mother whose child is now gone
What can I say to his family, what can I say to his advisor
What can I say to his brother, who has questions why he's the survivor
What can I say to conservatives that live in a world of rich hope
What can I say to liberals that constantly pimp the black vote
What can I say to these students whose tears I cannot dry
Whose questions I can't answer about why Demario had to die
What can I say to his teachers who encouraged him to be all he could be
What can I say to 20-year politicians that have brought no change we see
Be hurt but don't let it break you / Be angry but don't let it make you
Be confused but don't let it blind you / Be depressed but don't let it bind you
Be scared but don't let it hold you / Be furious but don't let it mold you
Be heated but don't let it control you / Open your heart and let God
console you
It's life and it's hard, Hold fast trust God
It's life and it's hard, Hold fast trust God

"You must get an education
        You must go to school
              And you must learn to protect yourself
And you must learn to protect yourself with the pen, and not the gun."
                                                    ~Josephine Baker

F.A.T.H.E.R.'S S.T.A.Y.

I grew up around the Elders
They became fathers when dad failed us
There were times when anger swelled us
Hating the men we looked like overwhelmed us

Times were frustrating full of pretending and phony
Mom was struggling and sometimes we went hungry
Not a lot of friends' times were lonely
Buster Browns and Tough Skins were on me so I looked homely

Friends playing catch with their dad, and I asked God where's mine
Broken on the inside, outside feeling fine
I wonder if he thought of me, I just wanted a little of his time
Where's the man that would groom me to see because I felt blind

Started seeing many women, never faithful in my flirt
My drug dealing, gang banging, strip clubs and all my dirt
But God spoke in the midst of all my hurt
Said, "You've tried everything, but only I work"

Stopped in my tracks, in the midst of the tears
Could I truly be a man with no man to hold near

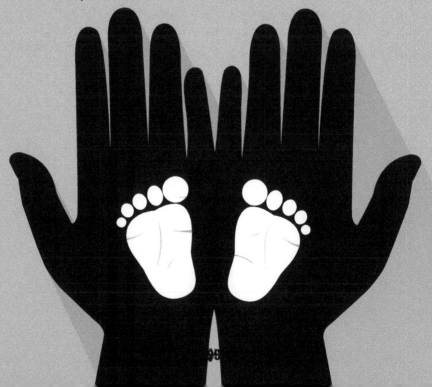

Could I grow up and start to see things clearer
Get over my fear and love this face in the mirror

He said, Son, you can. I'll empower you with my Holy Spirit
And He'll teach you how to be a man
See, I know your earthly father ran
But the Holy Spirit will teach you to stand
Engage yourself in my Word and learn my commands
I'll tap into your gift and empower you to take the land

One word, one rhyme, one child at a time
But it starts with you having a Christ-like mind
Seek after me, and destiny you will find
Just stay dormant for a while so I can help you unwind

See, your father was broken just like you
And the reason is his father was broken too
Give your life to me and I will remake ya
You'll be the curse breaker
And everything the enemy meant for bad I'll turn for your good
I'll raise you up as an example right in the hood

I'll take you beyond the best you can be
To take them corporate shackles off your feet and set you free
So you can be the father I created you to be
So your sons and daughters will see my power in thee

I'll send men like Elder Smith that teach the truth of my gift
I'll send men like Dr. Brazier that will lead you to the Savior
I'll surround you with men that love their wives
Men that trust God and pay their tithes
Men that for you will lay down their lives
Men that will let you know when they are hurt And won't wear a disguise

Men that will stand up against the wiles of the devil
Men that will teach you humility no matter what level
Men that will empower you to hold up your chest
To keep your chin up in failure if you did your best

And I'll bring your father back into your life
I'll put those shattered bones back together that were broken by strife
Everything wrong I'll make it right
And on his deathbed you'll have no regrets because I made it tight

I am the Father, when no one else bothered
When you ran the streets, I kept you from the slaughter
I am the Father, when you choose the wrong men
I protected your daughter
I am the Father, when you turned your back on me I just smiled
Because not even you can pluck you out of my hand once you're my child

I am the Father—humble yourself at my feet
Hear my word, wayward dads, you no longer have to be a deadbeat
Man up, go back to that child you've neglected
Ask for their forgiveness and let them know in me you've been resurrected
Repent for all those years you rejected and neglected
Endure their pain and you being disrespected
And watch the chains fall off
Watch me make their stony heart soft
Trust my word and see
That I'll make every day a Father's Day in me

Legacy

Sometime in 2014 a friend asked me...

"How many more young black men are going to die while you chase corporate dollars?"

I had no answer then, and I have no answer now
Torn between non-profit that pays no profit
And heavenly rewards that are great
Or living this tech life
Where at least I know rent and food and bills will be paid
And my family properly cared for
Still posting on Facebook and Twitter asking,
"The violence, when will we stop it?"
And then that same question comes to mind every time

*"How many more young black men are going to die
While you chase corporate dollars?"*

You'd think that'd be enough to make me holler,
But the blood that melds concrete red yells even louder
Because the color is not the paint that it came with
And in essence, I am no different from the hustler
See, they seek to make fast cash when I work 60 to 70 hours a week
Just to fill my tank with gas
To go back into this repetitive cycle of nothingness working for an employer
That tries to convince us it's for the kids
While at the same time I'm neglecting my own
And home has become a hotel; it's just a place I sleep
While the hustler has a corner
And it's just the place his customers he meets and greets
Until someone else comes along and creeps in to snatch his life away
After returning home at 10 pm after a 17-hour day I drive by yellow tape,
Where there are flowers and teddy bears and police officers and detectives
And a sheet, with news crews and a reporter, and some no teeth, nappy
braided character yelling into the camera,
"They didn't have to did my man like that!"

Ironically there's no eyewitness to this news, just another nigga dead because
African American is only for the politically correct
Another one I didn't reach
Another one to whom I didn't speak, another one I refused to teach
Because his look was menacing
And though I fear no man I have no time for drama
And maybe that's what his dad said to his teenage mother before he told her
I have no time for drama and left twice
The first time was walking away
Cut the second left an impression on a young black male
That he was worthy of no man's love
And that filled him with hate, and he thought no man deserved his love
The cycle continues in my hood
My city, where it's too expensive to move
To stay is too costly for your well-being, and there is no hero
Just old black politicians who for the sake of power
Would stay in office in their cancer-ridden bodies
Rather than train someone up younger than them because they think for a
minute, "They just might be better at this than me for this generation."
And I fear for the sake of comfort
I have left a generation paralyzed without hope
And as surely as history repeats itself, heroine is the new crack
While black women are our heroines in the community because
They realize without them the womb of this earth will be barren and fruitless
And if men don't stand up and climb flag poles
Then they have to do it on their own
Yes, Martin and Malcolm led the movement, but women infused it
There hails Tony Briscoe, a great technology leader
Living in his Highland Park house
who just made the cover of *Time* magazine's Leaders Today
While one of the young men he failed to mentor just made the cover
Of the *Chicago Sun-Times*, wanted for a triple homicide

Legacy

Somber

He is awake, paralyzed by stagnation
Wanting to wake up and live his dream
But it's not visible, tangible, no manifestation
Life, just dreary and slowly crawling

It's late, pouring hours into a job that has left him lifeless
Barren, friendless, visionless, hopeless
He sees the reflection in the mirror, and it is not his
It's a former life, of great faith and trust in the Lord

He smiles for a moment and thinks of a guy he once knew
A dreamer, hopeful, youthful, ready to take on the world
He misses that man and wishes he would once again visit with him
Tell him that he still believes he can dream, hope, trust, build

Scantily rhythms run syncopated over hollow shadows
Cracked surfaces pray for a little bit of rain so they can feel healed
Breathe, sing, before the sun scorches away that drop of sweetness
Leaving them dry, corroded, shattered, frozen

For a minute, he envisions being in that special place
His passion, his calling, his life, his lungs
But it's late and before he finds rest, the alarm clock sounds
Five years in, dreams forgotten, hope deferred has made his heart sick
He celebrates that life of joy his friends have that have taken that leap of faith
A report is due, he punches the clock, drinks the coffee of routine
Eats at the table of hesitation, and sees an RSS feed of his favorite Poet winning a Pulitzer . . .
. . . .that could have been me. . . . .

A PRAYER

I'm a bewildered man 'cause I think too much
Fear is my liquor, and I drink too much
They say, "Man, you got a wife and child that love you so;
You should be on cloud nine wherever you go"
But these cats don't know how I fight depression
Doin' all I can to survive life's lessons
But they can't look in my heart, can't look in my mind
'Cause they wealthy and fine while my bills fallin' behind
And I don't mean the bills that you pay; I mean the bills that you play
When it seems that life isn't going yo' way
In a church full of people, but it's only a few
That know I'm bleeding inside because their souls are true
You ever look in the mirror and wonder who's looking at you
I wonder if that cat knows what I'm going through
Started school at 35, got a long way to go
These city colleges, man, treat you like an animal
It really shouldn't be this hard to get in school
Wife told me disregard them fools and pay yo' dues
I feel in my heart that the Lord died for me
But my emotions seem to be havin' a negative effect on me
Can the sins of the father pass down to the son
Or that spirit of suicide; should I grab my gun
My wife is better off without me; should I get up and run
That man in the mirror said, "Dude, call on the Son"
But does the Father really wanna be bothered with me
See I got the Holy Ghost; why this problem following me
Think it not strange when those temptations arrive
Gotta keep it holy, that's the only way to survive
Porn used to have me, but I let that go
Now depression wants to grab me, can't fight no mo'
Wait a minute. Paul said endure as a good soldier

My wife on her knees, I can feel her prayers
I feel an angel hovering over; I know Jesus is there
But it's a lifelong battle between spirit and flesh
One that keeps blessin' and one that keeps stressin'
I'm trying to be a good man, take care of my fam
Keep my identity in Christ so I'll know who I am
When you ask what's wrong and I say I don't know
Don't walk away and close the door and say, "Whatever, bro"
Just pray for my fam and pray for my soul
'Cause I really love life, and I'm not trying to go
Got a wife to love and a daughter to raise
Got some kids that want to hear me lift up God in praise
So if you don't let this cup pass, Lord, I guess I gotta fight
Thanks for hearing my heart, Lord, I love you, good night

SIGNAL

No emotions were shown
Except that of a life that seemed simplistically happy
When I met her, we smiled; I remember the song she sang to heaven
Her voice—nice, lovely; a sparrow or humming bird with a silent whisper
I couldn't see her loneliness, I was jealous of her

She possessed a quiet quality of resolve
Assurance, energy, and calmness
If I could have seen pass my perception
Maybe I would have held a conversation with her

I would tell her how resilient she is
And she would tell me how broken she was
I would tell her that I loved the song she sang
And she would break out in tears and share her pain

I will hold her hand and pray for her
She would say, "Thank you for giving me a chance to live."
I would tell her that beauty is in the eye of the Creator
She would say "Endurer, you are genuine."

I would never see her again, well maybe
She would think of the moment we shared
Not friends, far from enemies
Just hearts trying to find a way to live life

I saw her again, we hugged; I held her as a brother would a sister
Then she disappeared, right in my arms,
My friends cried for the lives she touched

I wonder if I would have asked how she was beneath the smiles
Beneath the beauty, beneath the health
If I would see her again on this earth
She possessed a quiet quality of resolve
Then she dissolved from this realm without expectation
Without warning the sun went down

A cold element of loss picked up the pen
She wrote us a letter, but I will never read it
It would be too painful to remember
Or remind me of an opportunity
To look beyond physical strength and see inner wounds
It would remind me that I too am broken

GONE

MY LIFE HAS COME TO AN END
LEFT MY FAMILY AND MY FRIENDS
DON'T YOU WORRY; I'M NOT ALONE
BECAUSE MY LORD HAS TAKEN ME HOME

I KNEW THE DAY I WAS BORN
I WAS A DAY CLOSER TO DEATH
SO LET TEARS OF JOY RUN DOWN YOUR FACE
WHILE I REST IN A BETTER PLACE

REMEMBER THE JOY I GAVE
REMEMBER THE GRACE GOD GIVES
IF YOU COULD FEEL WHAT I FEEL NOW
SEEING MY MAKER, YES GOD LIVES

MY NEW LIFE WILL SOON BEGIN
I'LL SEE MY FAMILY AND MEET NEW FRIENDS
DON'T YOU WORRY; I'M NOT ALONE
I'M WITH MY MAKER IN A BETTER HOME

empty

I'm trying to find a way to embark on the journey of life
But find myself having no strength to do so
I am alone like an oasis in the desert
Thirsting for someone to break through the heat and touch me
The dew of nature soothes what is left little of the silence
Loud sounds peak through the eerie daylight trying to get a glimpse of hope
Swinging umbrellas serve another purpose of making men look cool
Locked in a den of egostical solace afraid to shed tears
Prism shades conceal the heart of iniquity only for a time
I am in danger of losing me jeopardizing the gift that allows me to breathe
I pulsate through memories that are etched out of my mind slowly
Remember how we were then, so pleasant and relevant, we were culture
Vanity looms in the mirror but frowns at the arrows flight
This is a moment of special caliber, whispers and betrayal
Complicated words brand confusion with expression
I have left them in silence, abstract, awkward, unfulfilled
I am pleased at their bewilderment questioning what I was speaking of
It keeps me at bay so they never see my tears, never see my pain
Never know my plight; never know why I smile often
I choose to be distant, in time, in space, in matter, existence is shattering
Their silence is my reward, but their joy is my jealousy
These men are free in chains, and I am bound in guilt
Did you hear that? My bow has been pierced
I am broken I am thirsty waiting for the one that can touch me
I remove myself from elements I am meant to be in solitude
They laugh at me and I am grateful for I know they are mortal
Frail, human, wicked and caring
Linger no more at the skies closing rainbow of monotone cartridges
We have touched the earth's core, it breathes for survival
And we kill her softly with hatred
Love slips away through the shattering of a glass
I am evasive, they are elusive
But we all are trapped, engaged, captured, framed
For all to see what isn't really there, fear is real
Because we give it power, choose life and forget ramblings that are empty

My Deck of Cards

How do I tame the dark within
I asked the Lord to give me this gift of the pen
So I can write and express what I feel therein
I can't live in the past, but memories surface again and again
How have I made it through all the hurt and all the pain
Even the sin through my life holding my head in shame
It's because Christ died for me, and now I'm changed
Took shackles off my mind so I wouldn't be deranged
Can you explain how others went through the same thang
But they became rapists and murderers and criminally insane
Not even my wife can dry the tears I cry
Only the Lord is safe for me to run and hide
Lord knows I've tried to write of His joy and all
But it's the truth that keeps me speakin' to y'all
It's His grace that lets me tell my life
It's His love that lets me share the Christ
It's His power that keeps me when I am weak
It's His mercy that covers me as I walk the street
Look deep in ya life while you're picking your brain
And you'll see how you overcame
Yeah it's real nice to know that Jesus walks
But I find it better to know that Jesus talks . . . to me
Through His Word, that's where I find my peace
For the dark within, it's the Holy Spirit that tames the beast
My love for the Lord will never cease
Through tests and trials, I pray my hopes never decrease
I hope to trust Him and that my faith increase
If my mind is stayed on Him, I'll be in perfect peace
I was dead without perfection while under the law
Now it's by God's grace and Christ's death, because I'm flawed
So it's only through Christ that I bring you my pain
'Cause He has taken all bad and made it my gain

WELCOME HOME

Welcome to America, land of the free, home of the brave
Where the cursed seeds of Africa stay,
Land of the bound, ghetto of the slave
Where masters wear black robes and the whip is a gavel
And every time it slams down another minority life unravels
Salty because of transatlantic travels, trying to find ourselves
And our culture is a never-ending battle

Welcome to America

Where athletes get billions and teachers get pennies
Where our daughters are stripping to pay for college
Because tuition fees are plenty
And thugs got pants sagging cause their hearts sagging
While mortuaries are basing projected summer earnings
Off young black males being toe tagged

Where sisters turn down brothers because they're educated but have no swag
And brothers turn down sisters because they're more educated
And feel their egos will be castrated
See we've been blinded by ambition
Where a man is judged by the size of his third leg and the car he drives
But it's the mental key that should turn his ignition

Welcome to America

Where we abort babies because it's convenient
Where NBC can edit God out of the Pledge of Allegiance
Then say, "Oops, we didn't mean it"
Where unemployment rates continue to rise and make our temperature boil

Where my soldiers are losing eyes legs and lives over oil
President telling us that things are getting better
Wake up brother, we are in turmoil

Yes, Welcome to America

Where the world gathers to call us mean
But when tsunamis and earthquakes hit we're the first ones on the scene
Despite our flaws and all we try to do the best we can
To reach down and help our fellow man, yes, Welcome to America

Welcome to America, where a drug dealer can build an empire state of mind
Where you can take 50 cents and flip 50 million in ten year times
Where even without a degree you can rise to the occasion
Where you can be free to marry a black/white/Asian or Caucasian

Welcome to America, where pastors that were long went wrong
Seducing black boys in thongs saying they speak from God's throne
Now find themselves alone
Hopefully, they're not far gone
And repentance will lead them to the true Throne

Welcome to America, where Republicans couldn't find Osama
And since they couldn't kill him they are trying to kill Obama
It's like Bush could do no wrong and Obama can do no right
And kids tease the intellectual black child by saying they're talking white
When they are actually speaking right

Where gas is going up and mileage is going down
Where Miss America can get fake breasts
But if they find nude pics they take her crown
Where babies kill babies over government-owned turf
Where men beat their women until they are blue like smurfs

Welcome to America

Where opportunity knocks at the door with those who have vision
Where they are finally sending the swindling Madoff's to prison
Where churches give plenty to the poor
Where we can serve the Lord freely without communists kicking in our door

Yes, welcome to America

Where we're inviting Satan in and etching God out
But we still raise our children on faith and not doubt
My country tis of thee, sweet land of liberty, no matter how far I've gone
I kick the heel of my Fodies because there's no place like home
She's mine forever, for worse or for better she'll be
My America, we sail till death from sea to shining sea

Blossom

A petal falls
Slowly from a rose
  You will never be forgotten
The sea's salt water was gracious
    Preserving memories that we'll hold dear forever

Life seemed but a moment
  But you lived that moment so strong
Striving to find life and joy
    In fatigue in pain
        It was your time and you whispered, "Let me go"

Passion brews in our hearts
        Your legacy of care and nurture moves on
Your struggles we've overcome
  We gaze in the corners of our mind
        Always hoping to catch a glimpse of your smile

The thorns are gone now
  You can be held in the arms of the Husbandman
The Love we know, nothing can separate

A fragile
  Frame will one day sprout up a glorious temple
The other side of the mountain
  holds treasures forever more

A small giant raises its threshold through the weeds
  New life can now breathe
I gasp at the loss but relish in what is to come
    we grieve heavy and cry with joy and a little sorrow
For we know the Eternal will care for you better than we
  Your legacy lives, life gives new wisdom
Ssssshhhhh, go to sleep, tomorrow will come

B.O.D.Y.
Bent On Destroying Yolks

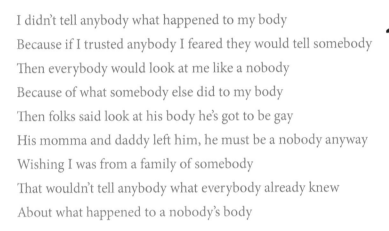

Growing up as a child I always wanted to be somebody
Even though in the IDA B they said we were nobody
I still had dreams of being somebody
Until somebody grabbed me and took my body
And made me feel like a nobody

I didn't tell anybody what happened to my body
Because if I trusted anybody I feared they would tell somebody
Then everybody would look at me like a nobody
Because of what somebody else did to my body
Then folks said look at his body he's got to be gay
His momma and daddy left him, he must be a nobody anyway
Wishing I was from a family of somebody
That wouldn't tell anybody what everybody already knew
About what happened to a nobody's body

I wondered if anybody knew the pain in my body
How my music teacher said I could play for everybody
The he started rubbing my hands on the keys while starring at my body
That's when music left me
And who could I tell
Because there wasn't anybody there for a nobody with a tainted body

How could somebody do that to anybody's body
I didn't know until I met somebody that was a nobody
That wanted to be loved by anybody and we were so close
Then we became each other's everybody
Until people looked at us like we were nobody
But it didn't matter because together two nobodys' made us somebody

But we knew this thing wasn't natural to be anybody
So with pain we separated and again became nobodys
With everybody telling somebody about how we used our bodys
I mean to do that you must be a nobody

Now look in the mirror and wonder if you are that somebody
That was talked about by everybody searching for love from anybody
All because you were a nobody because of what somebody did to your body
Now you're helping nobodys become somebodys
To reach everybody because of what happened to your body
So it will never again happen to anybody

And if somebody walked in your shoes they wouldn't tell anybody
Because of what everybody might say about a nobody
Who desired to help everybody
With a rest and trust in God because of what his Son endured in his body
So I can be . . . somebody

If I Be

If I be the man with no purpose in life
Then I be a man with no shame
For the path I have chosen is of my own accord
Therefore, I am the master of my fate

If I be the man who takes the life of another
Then I am a man aware of the consequences
For I have power over my victims
As the system that confines me has control of me

If I be a man who waits for the love of one
Then I be a foolish man
For good things come to those who seek
Not to those who sit and wait

If I be the man able to detect different states of mind
Then I am a man you should fear
For your mind, soul, and heart I can read
And your security of self is transparent

If I am a man of great love, then all who come to me I help
I assist them in any way deemed, for helping others brings me joy

If I be a man with a lost soul
Then I shall perish
So I'll be damned if I be

L
   e
      a
        v
          i
            n
              g

Dedicated to Nicole Cooley

I saw a tear fall from a rose and it was caught by the thorn
Hovering before it touched the ground it sang a song
Resonating of melancholy and joy
Breathing laughter and sorrow
Forever etched in the memory of hearts she touched
Friends she made, lives she inspired, hope she gave

The petals painted a road that was ever obscure
Yet pulsated from the stem its nutrients
Of care, sustenance, and contentment
Raising glasses for a toast but shattered when touched
Because we realize that life is delicate and fragile
Challenging and not always friendly, we smile at this vessel

That brought hope where despair visits
And change where complacency vacations
That tear finally let go so another could come afterwards
To make new heights, to carry on legacy
And empower a generation to believe

Many watched as it hit the ground
They clutched their hands, they held their hearts
They opened their arms and felt a splash called love
It was then the sun pierced through the clouds
The moon churned in the night

And Lord Byron arose to bid thee farewell
"Those smiles unto the moodiest mind their own pure joy impart
   Their sunshine leaves a glow behind that lightens o'er the heart"
.......I Saw You Weep

Breast Cancer

It came like a thief in the night, but it stayed till morning

Seeing and feeling this strange lump in my breast protrude while I stretched from yawning. And my visit to the doctor said not to worry, that it would probably be benign

But it was aligned with malignancy without contingency
This visitor was in me and it wasn't friendly—it was against me.

And now I am part of the struggle as I wrestle with this guest that metastases. And even with radiation and chemo in front of me, they say that it may not be cast aside.
So I told my husband, and I could tell he wasn't man enough to stay, seeing the weakness in his eyes

After two months, he left my side

So under the shadow of the almighty I decided to hide because loneliness and disease can prompt even the strongest to suicide. But I wanted this cancer to commit suicide and die knowing how bad it wanted to stay.

And the doctors told me to see an oncologist that told me I had to cut my precious joys away. How can this be? I am only 33, how will I breast feed this seed that is not even growing in me. And what will I do with my Victoria's Secret, because no one told me that Victoria's Secret was actually the silence of death. And that death was the silence that crept in my temple.

Live or die, the decision is quite simple

Make provisions for your incisions but put no fake ones on me. If I can't have that which was born me, then people will have to love the torn me alone because the one who said in sickness and in health was wrong for me.

But the God that spoke life into existence was strong for me

How long for me to be engaged with tragedy? The essence of my body sculpted by the Creator is now blasphemy. And kids are beautiful but

cruel cause they see me with no breasts and laugh at me.
And I cry inside because I have no one to laugh for me.

But I'm breathin'

Missing my twins will have me forever grieving,
but I'm living just enough for the city.
We are army strong
From Susan B. Komen to Relay for life
We stretch our arms across the county
Cause my stretch was too short
so this sisterhood of women became long for me
Teaching me that I don't have to endure hardness on my own
And together we could beat this cancer until it's gone

I am a survivor; I'm not gone give up

Cause the Destiny of my future Child has to live
So their child can live, so attention to this rage against the machine
can give assistance to bypass that which is drug resistant
to offset the malignant and bring back the natural tone of my pigment

We must never cease to be a force against the nature of this beast
And all those who fell before me are martyrs for the cause
as we champion for politicians to use their hearts
and depart from their sanctimonious laws
That would leave us on the outskirts without shirts to flirt with death
We stand unified until we're exhausted with nothing left
So those that continue to stay away because they feel we're contagious
Don't be outrageous because chances are you'll cross this journey too
And despite how you've treated us, we'll be there for you
Not to judge you but love you
Not to shove you but hug you
The pain will still be great but the work is greater
No time for haters
Cause cancer knows no color
It only knows itself
So put racism and religion on the shelf and reach out to help
Spread the love, spread the joy
We can empower change
We can empower healthier life styles
We can inspire hope
To rise up to this challenge together and cry

We won't stop fighting against cancer
Until we help cancer die
So baby cry, we are to help you through
And for those that left your side be encouraged
They just weren't strong enough to love all of you
Broken but not alone, neglected but not forsaken
We press on and move forward
We believe that victory is waiting
So my sisters, hold the line
Victory is here
We shall overcome
We shall be fine
We are more than survivors
We are History

I Made It

I made it—Because I surround myself with people who said I could
I made it—Because I surround myself with people who said I would
I made it—Because I surround myself with people who said I should
I made it—Because I'm more than a conqueror and survivor

Even with sleepless nights I managed to merge six classes
Like my name was MacGyver
My mom set the bar so high with love
That I had no choice but to go higher
See, before my dad left this world
He gave me a city and said, "Son, go and build and empire"

I made it
Sometimes had to move at a fast pace
Like the rabbit to jump over the hurdles
Had to exercise wisdom and be cautious
And slow down like the turtle
Had to be as cunning as a fox
When questions were transformed to try and trip me up
Had to be as wise as a serpent
When supporters where secretly trying to rip me up
And even if there were those that came in disguise
I didn't see them because God covered me
While I kept my eyes on the prize
Keep my mind on Him, and He saved me from the locust
Even took time for a little fun, but it's all good when you have focus

I made it
See I'm not one of the norm
My family raised me as a village, they cared so much I had no reason to see
The ways of the world and conform
See long before this medical degree came
I already had an MD behind my name
When others slouched I showed much dedication
When others quit I showed much determination
When others turned from God I showed much devotion in every situation
When others tattooed their body
I tattooed my heart with the Master's designation
I made it
When others blended in, I stood out in the crowd
When others did it for self, I did it to make my parents proud
Through sleepless months and countless exams

The God in me showed the me in Him who I am

I made it
For my children who knew daddy had things to do
Thank you for reminding me that my first ministry is you
Thanking Him for a faithful wife that supports the dream
Her I esteem because she put the T in our team

I made it—the journey doesn't end
I made it—I plan to reach back and help a friend
I made it—I plan to turn around and return the support to my kin
I made it—And even with my dad gone, every time I inhale
I can feel him breathing within

With loss, I made the gains come to life
With sorrow, I made joy from the plight
With hurt, I made peace from the pain
With heartaches, I made sunshine from the rain

Emotions had me stressed, but I found the blessings
Mistakes had me perplexed, but I learned the lesson
Anxiety had me unsure, but I stopped second guessing, ya see
And Fear, well, I had a praying mother, so that wasn't an option for me

See everyone has a mother, but I have one that is also a friend
And it's because of her sacrifices that I am blessed with the position I am in
So much love I received I couldn't even see the haters
I was destined to be great because I serve a master that is greater

And that is how I made it.

Dedicated to the Belin Family

Jesus encouraged me this morning to dream again
Told me to speak life to my heart and tell it to beat again
Said look back over those dead goals and plans
And tell them to breathe again

I want my wife to look back into my eyes
And see that beam again
See passion in my mind
And feel that steam again

I don't want to be depressed over defeat again
So my prayer is that me and fear never meet again
And if we do, no more soft shoes
I'm putting my cleats to him

For God knows the plans that He has for me
And if I start seeking His kingdom first, I'll feel Him expand in me
Season me with His grace so nothing tastes bland in me
Singing praises to Yaweh so loud you'd think there was a band in me

So I want to inspire you
Work hard on your plans till they perspire you
And if God didn't say it, let nothing retire you
Keep dreams alive until life expires you

Leave a legacy behind
So the world can grow on
Write that book on how you overcame rape, thoughts of suicide, molestation
So someone can be encouraged to go on
Put it in the hands of a rapper so he'll have something to flow on
Put it in the hands of a poet so they'll have something to do a show on
Put it in the hands of a pastor so they'll have something to preach on
Put it in the hands of a principal so they'll have something to teach on

Time to hope again
Time to build up that spiritual resilience so you can cope again
So you can say Hallelujah any how
When you're up against the ropes again
Time to write the vision and make it plain
So when satan distorts your thought,

You can read it to put it back in your brain
True soldiers know how to endure the pain
Crazy how it's only in Christ that loss becomes gain

Keep walking by Faith and not magical hocus pocus
You'll surely overcome the locust
Do your good deeds in secret, and God will take notice
Let the haters keep hatin'
You just stay focused

Keep pressin till the blessin is manifestin
And in the journey people will ask how you transformed
From smiling to stressing
And you can tell them I learn to live again
Instead of being selfish
I learned to live again
I learned to pray more (pause)
And instead of running away I learned to stay more
And instead of being intimidated
I learned to say more

Why, because I realized that God sees the best in me
What I thought was trouble was just Him testing me
Learned that in the trials He was just perfecting me
I wasn't consumed by the fire
Because He was protecting me
Holy Spirit power done resurrected me
The call of salvation has elected me
So I stand on the promises of God because they are true
So you should get to know Christ, because He already knows you

HOW LONG?

How long will chains remain shackled to my brain?
While I wrestle with parts of my flesh that my spirit hasn't tamed
How long will my stress prevail and my prayers fail?
After years of travail, how long will I be in the valley?

How long will I get smiles from crooks while saints give dirty looks?
These chains remain shackled over my mind
So how long will I walk spiritually blind?
How long till I have peace at home,
where I've allowed the enemy to set up his throne?
Where mercy flows with no will,
love kills and suffering seems to last forever
Joy comes in the morning, but the years of my life have all been nights
Too tired to walk up the hill, why am I still in this valley?

Years of tears and broken dreams plagued by low self-esteem
In the mirror I see a reflection of the inner me that longs for peace
That longs for love,
That longs to be embraced
by the face of victory and not oppression

Yet my prayers have failed; in vain I have travailed
In my mind once again the enemy has prevailed
How long will I dance with no music,
will I sing with no song,
will I live with no peace at home?

How long will I look to the hill and scream
And hear no answer echo in my valley?
How long will night be my day and days be night and fear cancel my faith?
How long will I walk by sight in the valley?

Why am I still in this fire holding onto keys that don't belong to me?
When will my warrior's whine become a Warrior's Cry
Where the true intercessors lie?
On their face for saints who are bound by the wiles of the enemy
How long will I carry burdens that turn my spine to Ahab
And turn my heart to Jezebel?
In this valley where the trees are too high
To hear intercessors cry for release and peace
More peace and release from ungodly soul ties

That seek to destroy the spirit I employ
How long will night be my light and darkness be my sight?
Where I have no will to fight and depression is my only right
How long will this furnace of affliction be my drug addiction?
My only high is wondering why I'm in this valley unable to die

Who's there? Jesus is that you?
Or has deception given me a false impression of a spiritual rescue?
Are those angels I see coming at me?
Or are they demons with more schemes to corrupt my beautiful dreams?

How long will I say I've received a word from thee?
When I can't discern if it's from the enemy or me
How long till my inner me becomes one with thee?
When can I flee this valley?

How long will I bless others and I remained stressed?
How long will I sow good seed and reap only greed?
My tears scream to be dried while my hands remain tied
How long will I be tried in this valley?

This valley where hope has no face and prayers go unanswered
This valley where childhood things
Corrupt my adult mind with horrible thoughts
This valley where deliverance has no reach and suffering clings like a leech
This valley where I cry and my only high is wondering why I'm unable to die
How long will this valley be my throne?
How long, Lord?
How long until your mountain becomes my home?
How long will my peace be in a land beyond reach?
And my prayers be on hold
Because of strongholds that have taken lock on my soul

I long to be released from the belly of this beast, this affliction
This valley where trees allow me to breathe but won't allow me to see
Where wind doesn't blow, where water doesn't flow and miracles don't show
Where prosperity won't grow and Shekinah won't glow

This valley where the furnace of affliction is my drug addiction
And my only high is wondering why I'm in this valley unable to die
How long, Lord, Father, Savior, Friend, Master, Deliverer?
Do you hear me?
How long till I leave this valley?

Journey

You'll encounter emotions yet remain content
You'll have difference of opinion with no conflict
You'll have tears in prayer but prevail
Knowing that the effectual prayers of the righteous availeth much

You'll have friends with no cliques
You'll have opinions with no division
You'll have hugs with no motives
Confess your faults one to another and exhort each other daily

You'll encounter grief with no sorrow
You'll witness attitudes with no anger
You'll have trials with no failure
All things work together for those who are in Christ Jesus

You'll leave a comfort zone but remain home
You'll separate from loved ones but not from covenant
You'll enter a foreign land but possess its prosperity
The riches of the wicked are laid up for the righteous

You'll be tempted and pass the test
You'll be persecuted and rejoice
You'll be mocked and remain steadfast
Upon this rock you will build my church

You'll be praised and stay humble
You'll be exhorted and stay abased
You'll be honored and I'll be glorified
And I will give you favor among men

Lo, I'll be with you always

Reflections

Hollow trees make sounds that bring back autumn's memories
Does hope still spring eternal?
Shallow breezes blow leaves past your walks
And you know you've visited here before
Dreams bring past moments that make you awake in tears
Then you realize

I am not gone

Country roads ripple over the morning dew
Crickets sing into the heart of grief
Does hope still spring eternal?
Silence falls as cotton
A subtle whimper breaks the field's code of quietness
The moon descends into the shadows of time
The sun lays dormant under the clouds' rain
As life strikes at the soul of man
Winter takes its place in eternity's arms

A silhouette of thoughts invades your tension
And laughter begins to shake hands with sorrow
Will I be able to make it in future tomorrows?
No answer, no warning, just the rhythm of....
A love not lost but in transition
To a rhythm all humanity will pulse to

I awake to a kiss on the forehead
A rubbing of the tummy
A baby starring into the eyes of a strange but safe creature
Waves cover the sands
And I still dance with you, hold hands with you
I would give anything to take one last glance at you

Hope rests within the soul
Wake up my love
Ease your heart, calm your fears
Look in the mirror . . . I am still here

Unchosen Affection

It wasn't that she wanted to be gay, but men ripped her to shreads
Innocence lost as a child because grown men forced her into bed
And for the 3 men that raped her, for each 1, five women showed her loved
And for the 3 men that raped her, for each 1, 10 women gave her hugs

It wasn't that she didn't like men, it's just women treated her better
See the men in her life treated her cold, but the women gave her a sweater
And for every man that walked out of her life, a woman wrote her a letter
And for every man that blacked her eye, a woman gave her a kiss
And for every man that forgot her birthday, a woman became her wish

And for every man that choked her, a woman gave her a massage
And for every man that gave her little, a woman gave her a collage
And for every tear they made her cry, a woman wiped them away
And for every man that kicked her out, a woman provided her a place to stay

It wasn't that she didn't like men, it's just women just treated her better
And for every storm caused by a man, a woman became her umbrella
It wasn't that she wanted to be gay, but men ripped her to shreads
Innocence lost as a child because grown men forced her into bed

And for every man that called her ugly, a woman said she was pretty
And for every man that called her dumb, a woman said she was witty
And for every man that made her numb, a woman made her feel
And for every man that bruised her body, a woman helped her heal

It's not that she wanted to be gay, but women just loved her better
And for every man that walked away from her, a woman would be forever
It's not that she didn't like men, but women just made her whole
And after a while men just didn't appeal
And of herself she gave women her soul

Where Is My Father?

Father, have you seen the violence in these streets
Can you smell the scent of blood and how it reeks
I mean I serve you daily
But every Monday when I get to school I'm burying a friend
And my friends used to be scared to go outside the house
Now they are scared to sit by the window and relax on the couch
See where I'm from the Folks and the Mo's breed terror
And the police don't make it better
Cause I watch them drive by drug dealers
While they are waiting to catch the big-time peddlers

And while they are conducting their five-year investigations
The deaths are multiplying in our community
See we speak a lot about black love
When there ain't a lot of black unity

And in all this I ask, Where is my heavenly Father?

And from Oscar Grant to Travyon Martin
It seems like no justice no peace
But the licensed killers have my brother deceased by carrying a piece
Mothers are no longer raising their babies to fit caps n gowns
They made decisions to see if their sons coffins will be black or brown

See where I'm from, walking in Terror Town can get you stomped out
And cruising through Englewood too slow
Can get you shotgun pumped out
Even the young daughters that turned into following a bad trend
Trading in self-respect
Following MC Lyte's suggestion and choosing a ruff neck

And in all this I ask, Where is my heavenly Father?

Six-year-olds being gunned down on porches
Gun violence so violent
But the biggest perpetrator of all is our silence

Too scared to stand up because they say snitches get stitches
But how will they be cowardly
And allow cemeteries to keep digging ditches
And it's hard to explain to a mother that God is number one

When she's asking, then why did God allow the death of my third son

See the streets are too full of A.R. Leaks
And the survival of the young black male just looks bleak

So I ask, Where is my heavenly Father?

Cause my soul is breaking and my heart is aching
Too many lives being taken and too many leaders faken
Tell us to pray but there is no action, so save yo drama
Cause the innocent are being killed, so I have no more love for Karma

See, where I'm from the high schools host gang fights
And corners host meetings
And being in the wrong hood without consent
Can get your teeth embedded in cement

See where I'm from, girls give oral sex at age ten
And spread legs at age twelve
And for them, the psychology of hood life only exists at stage Hell
Pregnant at fourteen by a punk that is tattooed out
And she only understands silence when he gives her a fist to the mouth

And the country, well they just want us incarcerated
For some reason we have believed that life in prison is overrated
But the extinction of the black man is his presence
From the home being confiscated
In a cell with another man forcing their relationship to become conjugated

See where I'm from, the chance of me to live
Is as small as the opportunity for college
And my 4.0 average means nothing if it doesn't match my street knowledge
See where I'm from
It's hard to tell people to have belief in a Lord
that can save
Cause while I am spitting this piece
Another mother is preparing for tomorrow's service
Putting her son in a grave

And she only has one question, Where is my heavenly Father?

Nature

There is a whisper that echoes around mountaintops
And shakes loose snowcaps, leaving bruises on hearts
Buried under avalanches of scars she never realized
Until the death of her mother
Now at 30 years old, she seeks to unfold these tears
That are more than remorse or grief
But stem from erupting volcanoes
And each level of magma burns through decades of emotions
She kept encrusted under layers of memories
That once helped her sleep in peaceful ashes

Now she stands frozen in an ice cap
Looking up in a coffin that is no longer buried at this moment
She finally believes in resurrection
Her joy of the tricycle that Dad bought her when she was three
Became a nightmare
When she dreams at age thirteen
Of being sexually aroused only to wake up
And find her father sucking on her overly developed breast
And the taste of Wild Irish Rose on his tongue,
She knew two things from that time
One, she'd never love another man again
And two, alcohol would not be her healing drug
That night the ambulance came
To remove his body from their mother's room
They thought her screams came from losing dad
But they actually came from knowing dad in a biblical sense
Non-existent anymore
And her last memory of him would leave her scarred forever
But not more than the words of the maternal who gave her life
"You little whore"
His act of sin gave him a heart attack while her heart was under attack
And it simply doesn't beat anymore
That night her mother threw her out of the house
And it was fine because she never cared for sleeping in cemeteries

Pacing patiently with blood basking down her sorrowful soul
She silently weeps wounded wondering
Why all these zombies have returned with no warning
She realizes she's still thirteen inside and seventeen years later
Rummaging through her mother's pictures

She hasn't seen since she departed
Holding an image of her glass family
A brief smile cracks her soul, and she looks up
And her younger sister walks into the room
"It's good to see you, sis. It's been too long"
She embraces her sibling and thinks to herself
"I guess dad did something right"

LIFE TO LEGACY LLC

Let us bring your story to life! Life to Legacy offers the following publishing services: manuscript development, editing, transcription services, ghostwriting, cover design, copyright services, ISBN assignment, worldwide distribution, and eBooks.

Throughout the entire production process, you maintain control over your project. Even if you have no manuscript, we can ghostwrite your story for you from audio recordings or legible handwritten documents. Whether print-on-demand or trade publishing, we have publishing packages to meet your needs. We make the production and publishing processes easy for you.

We also specialize in family history books, so you can leave a written legacy for your children, grandchildren, and others. You put your story in our hands, and we'll bring it to literary life!

Please visit our website:
www.Life2Legacy.com
Or call us at:
877-267-7477
You can also e-mail us at:
Life2Legacybooks@att.net